Revolt in the South

Revolt in the South

by Dan Wakefield

GROVE PRESS, INC. • NEW YORK
EVERGREEN BOOKS LTD. • LONDON

62941

To My Mother and Father

and

To Murray

My sincere thanks to *The Nation* magazine, which enabled me to make several trips to the South over the past five years. Portions of this material have appeared previously in *The Nation*.

—D. W.

Contents

Foreword: America and the South

In the same way that it is the illusion of the South that it 'knows' the Negro, it is the illusion of the North that it has set him free. Both camps are deluded.

—James Baldwin

This fight will not end until every Negro, whether in Chicago or Jackson, Mississippi, can be treated as a first-class American citizen.

—A Negro student sit-in leader
from Nashville, Tenn.

On a hot September morning in 1955 I sat in a Jackson, Mississippi, hotel room talking on the telephone to Robert "Tut" Patterson, a former Mississippi State football star who had recently founded the first chapter of the White Citizens Councils. Mr. Patterson had not long before been interviewed for the first time by a "Yankee Reporter"—Homer Bigart, then of the *New York Herald Tribune*, and one of the best newspapermen in the country—and was quoted in the lead of the story as informing Mr. Bigart that "This is not the United States of America; this is Sunflower County, Mississippi."

I was anxious to visit that sovereign province myself, but Mr. Patterson assured me he would have no more of Yankee reporters and wouldn't see me if I came. He did, however, inform me over the telephone in tones that could have probably been heard from Jackson to Sunflower County without the aid of Alexander Graham Bell that "There won't be any integration in Mississippi. Not now, not 100 years from now, maybe not 6,000 years from now—maybe never."

Later that day I gained an audience with W. J. "Bill" Simmons, Mr. Patterson's emissary in Jackson, who gave me the same assurances in person, along with some details on how the newly-formed White Citizens intended to make good the claim. On every return to the South in the following years I heard the same theme, and despite the few scattered voices of opposition from "moderate" whites, and the weary, waiting voices of local Negro leaders, the voice that rose above all the rest was the chant of the white segregationist, repeated like a litany that held the whole South in its rhythm: *"We're just not gonna do it."*

Against that theme, beneath it, almost muted in patience and the weariness of long frustration were the voices of the so-called "extremists" of the local NAACP in the Southern towns and cities who spoke most often in the even tones of George Ferguson, the NAACP president in Charlottesville, Virginia, who sat in his living room in 1956 just after the school integration order for his city had been postponed and quietly told me, "We've waited a long time; we can wait a little more." He, and others like him, spoke with calm assurance and conviction of eventual victory, but their words seemed drowned beneath the overriding hymn of the white majority.

Then, this Easter, I heard the new voice that had risen in the South, speaking a different message. It was the voice of the Negro student sit-in demonstrators who had gathered from every state in the South at Shaw University to carry forward the movement for full equality they began in February at segregated dime store lunch counters and developed into a widespread movement that is both non-violent and non-compromising. The new voice was one of young men like Billy Smith, a student from Greensboro, North Carolina, who stood on the campus at Shaw explaining what was going on to some visitors and said of the movement he was part of: "Nothing can stop us."

That is the theme of the new movement that has suddenly changed the whole rhythm of the conflict in the South; the voice that chants "We're just not gonna do it" no longer is solely dominant; there is now the opposing and powerful voice that says just as firmly, "Nothing can stop us."

The first sound of each of those voices marked, respectively, the beginning and the end of a particular, definable period in our history. A. Philip Randolph has often said that the current struggle for equal rights is the modern continuation of the racial revolution in America that the Civil War began and left unfinished. Although this revolution never stopped (but sometimes, indeed, moved backward, as in the passage of the Jim Crow laws that followed Reconstruction), its first great modern phase

—the phase in which it was brought out into an open, and even foremost place, in American life— was set off by the Supreme Court decision of May 17, 1954, which held that segregation in the public schools was unconstitutional; that the segregated concept of "separate but equal" on which we had long been operating was a contradiction in terms. That set the stage for the battle, but did not, in reality, begin it. For the first few months that followed the historic day that the segregationists marked on their calendar as "Black Monday" there was mainly silence; it was a time like the one that separates the moments when a person is burned and when, in the fraction of a second that it takes for his body to absorb and react to the pain, he opens his mouth and screams. The scream, and the real battle, began two months later when Robert "Tut" Patterson and his white friends in Sunflower County, Mississippi, started the resistance movement of the Citizens Council and uttered their new Rebel yell that was taken up all through the South: "We're just not gonna do it." Despite the pressure of the NAACP and of the federal government, the segregationists largely maintained the upper hand, and their doctrine of resistance was accepted as the doctrine of "The South." As the Southern editorial pages so often pointed out, real social change must come from within—and both the NAACP (guided by the Negroes and white liberals of the North) and the various arms of the federal government could be labeled as "outside forces" seeking a basic change in an area whose citizens opposed such change. But the non-violent movement of Negro students that exploded last spring was a movement from within the South itself; it could not be ascribed to the Judges of the Supreme Court or the hand of the NAACP. In desperation, many segregationists (joined almost alone by Harry Truman) proclaimed that it was all the doing of the Kremlin. Probably the best answer to these allegations of "Communist inspiration" was made by the Rev. Martin Luther King, who simply pointed out that "If somebody is standing on my neck, I don't need Khrushchev to come over and tell me that somebody is standing on my neck." The sit-down movement originated in neither New York nor Moscow, but Greensboro, North Carolina. It came from, and spread through the South itself—reminding the nation and the world that "The South" does not mean merely the whites who live there, but the Negroes as well, and that these Negroes, too, are "Southerners"; that they, too, speak for "The South." When they spoke this spring to say that "Nothing can stop us" in the fight for full equality they ended the phase of that struggle that was dominated by the white segregationists. Their revolt began the second phase of the modern revolution in race relations in America.

Within that first period (the period that began with the declaration of the White Citizens in July, 1954, and ended with the declaration of Negro student demonstrators assembled at Shaw University on Easter, 1960) the major forces, pressure groups, philosophies, rhetoric, and tactics of the current racial revolution took shape and substance. Whatever happens now will be based on, and grow out of, the events of that time. And that is what this report is about. It does not pretend to be comprehensive, but, rather, aims to convey some understanding of the reality of that already receding era, through the faces and words and troubles of people who played a part in it, in the hope that such an understanding will not only help to illuminate events of that recent past, but also the events of the future that even now are growing out of it.

During that period I made five trips to the South on reporting assignments for *The Nation* magazine, and in the course of those assignments met and talked with white and Negro citizens in Sumner and Jackson, Mississippi; Norfolk and Charlottesville, Virginia; Montgomery and Tuskegee, Alabama; Atlanta, Georgia; Little Rock, Arkansas, and Raleigh, North Carolina. It is out of these experiences that I write.

I do not, and cannot, write as a "Southerner," for I was born in Indianapolis, Indiana, and I live in New York City. I hope, however, that I do not write as a "Northerner" either, in the sense of those comfortable folks who sit in Detroit or New York or Des Moines and look at the tragedies and struggles below the Mason-Dixon line with clicking tongues and ruffled sensibilities, regarding it all as the doings of naughty and un-enlightened neighbors who live outside the pale of the northern racial millenium. Such people are not only hypo-

crites, but moral voyeurs who stimulate their own
self-righteousness by looking at pictures of mobs in
the South and imagining that what they see is al-
together a "regional" problem that they, in the
North have solved. That is not the eye that I hope
to bring to these events. My aim is not to see them
as a "Southerner," or a "Northerner," but as an
American—and, most hopefully, as a human being.

The attempt to view the racial struggle in any
section of the country as basically an American,
rather than a sectional concern, should certainly not
be a novel notion in 1960. Yet even now, on the
eve of the centennial of the Civil War, citizens both
North and South tend to regard the Mason-Dixon
line as some moral equivalent of the Great Wall
of China. Northerners use the idea to feed their
illusion that racial injustice is, like cotton, a pe-
culiarly Southern product, and that if it weren't
for the South everything would be all right. Southerners use it to argue that racial injustice in the
South is "their own business," and, like any other
business, ought not to be interfered with by outsiders.

Many of the Southerners who use this argument
use it of course as a means of maintaining the status
quo, but there are others who sincerely believe in
equal rights and honestly feel that the South's fight
to achieve them is a private sectional concern.
William Faulkner, through his character Gavin
Stevens in the novel *Intruder in the Dust*, eloquently
expressed this view by saying that ". . . the injustice is ours, the South's. We must expiate and

abolish it ourselves, alone and without help or even (with thanks) advice."

But the best argument against this position that racial injustice in the South is strictly a "southern problem" is stated also by Gavin Stevens in the same dialogue, when he says that ". . . he [the Negro] has the capacity to endure and survive but he will not be thrown back decades and what he survives to may not be worth having because by that time divided we may have lost America." Note that Mr. Faulkner, a native Mississippian, through his character Gavin Stevens, also a native Mississippian, does not say the danger is of losing "The South," but of losing America.

The Northerner who thinks of the racial conflict as basically a Southern, rather than an American dilemma, thereby handily blinds himself to the fact that the segregation system of the North is different in form, but not in essence and outcome, from the system of the South. When the novelist James Baldwin, a Negro who was born in Harlem, went South last year to write about the land that his parents had left, he observed in his "Letter from the South" in *Partisan Review* that "segregation is official in the South and unofficial in the North, a crucial difference which nevertheless does nothing to alleviate the lot of most northern Negroes." The social principle of Negro inferiority underlies the life of Northern ghettos as well as the life of any Southern town.

It is often easy for the northern white to avoid confronting this reality, however, for he has set up a complex machinery to manufacture the illusion of equality. In New York City, for example, he can point to Negro participation in local politics, and proudly allude to the fact that a Negro, Hulan Jack, was elected Borough president of Manhattan. Of course, once Hulan Jack got the job, it became as "segregated" as the job of pullman porter on the New York Central. By the curious workings of the northern racial setup, it has become sheer "bigotry" to suggest that any citizen other than a Negro hold that office. As Murray Kempton remarked in the *New York Post*, "A white man can't become Borough President of Manhattan, and a Negro can't get an apartment on Central Park West."

The ghetto system of housing in the North has so far allowed it to look with aloof disdain at the furor in the South over school integration, because in most northern cities—especially in the wealthier neighborhoods—housing restrictions effectively prevent the possibility of large scale integration in the public schools. New York City has met this challenge by beginning in certain places "transfusions" of Negroes from crowded slum areas into better equipped schools in nearby white neighborhoods. And the parents of the white school children have often met this artificial integration with protests and picketing, as they did last year in the borough of Queens. The picketing parents of New York differed from the angry white parents of Little Rock only in their lower level of violence and their higher level of hypocrisy.

The New York parents did not speak of white supremacy; nor, in fact, did they mention the word "Negro." They merely protested the bringing in of "outside elements" to their schools. Mr. Baldwin observed of the difference for a Negro in segregation in the North and the South that "It is the etiquette that is baffling, not the spirit." Certainly it is only a question of "etiquette" that separates the southern segregationists who say they don't want Negroes in their children's schools from the New York mothers who fight the same battle but omit the word "Negro" from their picket signs.

So the North has watched this new era in the racial revolution in America in the way that it watched the revolt in Hungary—a highly significant, but very far distant conflict. To the northern white the battle of Little Rock, like the battle of Warsaw, was shameful, heroic, important, and remote. But now that era, too, is over. It ended with the conference of Negro student sit-in demonstrators at Shaw University this Easter.

It ended then because the mass movement that was born there has as its goal not merely the destruction of any one aspect of discrimination in any one area, but "full equality" for Negroes throughout America. As the Rev. Martin Luther King pointed out at that conference, the movement began in North Carolina, a state that has "a little" integration, and showed that the new generation of Negroes was not satisfied with that, or with anything less than the full equality guaranteed by the constitution—a document which the Negro students take to mean what it says. The student leader from Nashville who addressed the conference pointed out that the revolt he and his friends were part of would not be finished until Negroes in all America—in Chicago, as well as in Jackson, Mississippi—could be treated with full equality.

So this new revolt begun by the students is a southern movement in the sense that it started in the South, but an American movement in the sense that what it is fighting to destroy thrives in every section of the country. It began in the South, but it can hardly end there.

This report then is not about the South because of any illusion that the South is the only part of the country that has yet to solve the problem of racial injustice. It is about the South because the South is now the center of the struggle, the center of the open revolt against the federal government to maintain segregation, and also the new revolt of the Negroes to end it. It is likely that there, in the South, where this torturous conflict is being fought out in the open, without the protective cover of hypocrisy and polite evasion that overlays the North, that any solutions to our greatest American dilemma may finally come. Let us who live outside of it bear this in mind as we look at the South. Its hope is our hope, and its tragedies our own.

Chapter 1

White Law and Order

Beneath the gold draperies that canopy the long, high-ceilinged stage of the Montgomery, Alabama, City Hall sat the officers of the local White Citizens Council and their honored guests—the top officials of the city, county, and state police forces. Montgomery Safety Commissioner L. B. Sullivan, who heads the police and fire departments of this city of roughly 70,000 white and 50,000 Negro citizens, stood at the rostrum and told his appreciative public audience:

> Since the infamous Supreme Court decision rendered in 1954, we in Montgomery and the South have been put to a severe test by those who seek to destroy our time-honored customs. . . .
>
> I think I speak for all the law-enforcement agencies when I say we will use all the peaceful means at our disposal to maintain our cherished traditions.

So stand the police of Alabama—on the side of law, order and the cherished traditions of the white citizens. Indeed, the topic of this particular meeting in April, 1960, was "A Salute to Law and Order." I attended it with a young man and woman who live in Montgomery, and we sat throughout the proceedings in silence, neither clapping nor rising from our seats during the several standing ovations. Throughout the speeches I was taking notes, and this, along with our failure to rise and applaud at appropriate moments, was evidently enough to brand us as "outsiders." When we walked toward the door at the end of the meeting a middle-aged man in a brown business suit followed along beside us and began to shout at me, "Did you get enough information? I hope you got all the information you wanted!"

I said yes, thanks, I had all the information I wanted. He continued to follow, shouting and pointing at us, and other people began to stop and stare. He yelled out, "I know who you are! I know who all three of you are!"

By the tone of his voice and the look on his face, he seemed to be under the impression that we were, at the very least, three of the Four Horsemen of the Apocalypse. I extended my hand and told him my name, but he drew back and shouted, "Never mind, I know who you are! You're not welcome here!"

We walked on out of the door, and when we got to the street, several young sport-shirted men and one elderly white citizen fell in behind us. We walked on in silence to the car, which was parked around the corner from the City Hall, across the street from the fire station. Not looking back, we seated the girl in the car. I got in next to her by the door, and the other young man walked around to get in the driver's seat. Before we got in, my door was yanked open and two of the men who had followed us were grabbing at me, cursing and trying to pull me out of the car. They grabbed for my arms, legs, and the notebook and papers I carried, tearing at my clothes and ripping my jacket.

The young man who had come to the meeting with me quickly hustled the girl out of the car. She ran across the street to the fire station, where four or five Montgomery city firemen were standing outside watching us. She ran toward them yelling for help, and they hurried inside, retreating into a back room of the fire station, refusing to answer when the girl pounded on the door.

My own shouts by now had become quite loud and sincere, and the zealous citizens, who still had not managed to pull me out of the car, finally ran off down the street and out of sight. My two friends got back into the car, and just before we drove away the firemen appeared again outside the fire station across the street. They were smiling at us. Evidently they too were unmoved by, or unaware of, the doctrine of the uses of "peaceful means" in preserving tradition that their boss, Safety Commissioner Sullivan, had espoused in behalf of himself and his men at the meeting a few minutes earlier.

In fairness to the inspired citizens who attacked us, however, it ought to be explained that the Citizens Council "Salute to Law and Order" program was not exactly a Gandhian conference on the merits of love and non-violence, and L. B. Sullivan's text was far from being The Sermon on the Mount. One of the significant and dangerous features of the respectable racism practiced by the White Citizens Councils is that, although their leaders and orators never fail to mouth a firm dedication to law and order at every public gathering, they also stir the passions of their crowds with provocative and outraged attacks on all those who oppose their principles, and deliver soul-searing declamations on the sacred cause of white supremacy. If zealots leave these meetings and vent their passionate dedication to the cause by violent means, the Citizens Council officials can, of course, deny responsibility by citing their statements upholding "legal, peaceful means" of action.

Safety Commissioner Sullivan, for instance, could disclaim any incitement to violence in his speech by pointing to his clearly stated belief in "peaceful means" of preserving the threatened white traditions. But after that affirmation (a not too radical stand for a city police chief), he got down to more alarming matters. The City of Montgomery, he explained to his audience, was selected long ago as "a site for racial agitators and troublemakers to attack our cherished way of life." The pressure had increased of late, he said, because of the efforts of civil-rights groups to influence politicians in Congress and in the coming Presidential elections. The rabble rousers had so far met with little success, he reported, but there were dangers ahead:

Not since Reconstruction have our customs been in such jeopardy. . . . We can, will and must resist outside forces hell-bent on our destruction. . . .

As if this weren't enough to inflame the breast of any loyal white citizen, Mr. Sullivan went on to state: "We want these outside meddlers to leave us alone"; then, in a slow, meaningful tone of irony: *"If they do otherwise, we'll do our best to 'accommodate' them here in Montgomery."*

And who could say that the citizens who shortly afterwards attacked us were not just doing their best to "accommodate" some "outside meddlers?"

The audience had also been informed that outsiders were the real cause of the attempted Negro prayer march to the steps of the state Capitol on March 6, 1960, which barely was prevented from turning into a riot when an angry mob of 5,000 whites assembled to stop the demonstration. Program chairman Don Hallmark of the Montgomery White Citizens Council told the meeting that "The people who sponsored this demonstration were disappointed—they had a lot of money in it."

The Citizens Council "Salute to Law and Order" was held to honor the law-enforcement officials for their work in dispelling the mob and preventing violence at that demonstration. But one of the important groups that took an active part in controlling that explosive situation was not represented on the platform along with the city, county, and state police officials feted by the Council. This was the group of armed horsemen whose appearance on the scene marked a new addition to the law-enforcement procedures of the South. The band of mounted "deputies," led by Sheriff Mac Sims Butler, was composed of wealthy cattlemen from the surrounding area who now are on call for emergencies, and have several times come into town with their horses in trailer trucks for "civil defense" drills. During the prayer-march demonstration, they roughed up and threatened three press photographers, two from Alabama papers and one from Magnum of New York. One of the photographers was arrested for refusing to obey an officer (deputy) who told him to move back. These non-uniformed mounties are unknown by face or name for public record, and have been especially vigilant in preventing any pictures being taken of them.

Reasons of secrecy no doubt prevented them from appearing on the Citizens Council platform to share the honors with the city, county, and state police, but perhaps that was all for the best. The volunteer horsemen might well have been disappointed at the public's appreciation of their efforts. An estimated 5,000 of their fellow white citizens had turned up to form the mob that they helped to hold in tow on March 6; but not more than fifty sat scattered in Montgomery's large City Hall on "Law and Order" night. When Don Hallmark stepped to the front of the stage to open the meeting, he looked around the nearly vacant auditorium and asked: "Where is everybody?"

The only answer was an uneasy shifting as necks craned around at empty rows, and Mr. Hallmark, after asking those scattered at the back and the sides to come on down front and center, attempted to dispel the momentary gloom with a hopeful appraisal that "We think we make up for numbers in quality here. . . ."

It is easier to assemble larger numbers of white citizens for a mob than for a meeting. But that is not hard to understand—a mob at least offers excitement, but even the most ardent white supremacist must at this stage be weary of the ceremonies of the Citizens Councils. It is now six years since the conception of the W.C.C. sprang full-blown from the forehead of Robert "Tut" Patterson in Sunflower County, Mississippi, and with occasional and usually minor variations, the meetings of these defenders of the faith throughout the South remain as unchanged in rhetoric and style as high school graduation ceremonies.

As is the usual custom at these proceedings, chairman Hallmark harangued the conscience of his audience on the need for financial as well as moral support of their principles (last year Alabama's white citizens coughed up only $4,000 for the cause, while their brothers in Mississippi gave $160,000). In the same familiar formulas, Mr. Hallmark reaffirmed the organization's principles ("states' rights," "segregation," "preservation of our cherished customs") and its unbending allegiance to them ("despite federal prisons or anything else, no force can make us integrate").

It was Safety Commissioner Sullivan who provided the only new notes in the evening's incantations. If there were any skeptics present who had doubted the feelings of the police about their role in quelling the mob at the prayer-march, Mr.

Sullivan soothed their minds. He complimented the mob for its "cooperation" with the law-enforcement officials by finally dispersing without drawing blood, and made it clear that the police had not only been there to preserve the peace, but to preserve the white traditions as well. "Spring is here, and birds are singing," Mr. Sullivan said, "but with the help of our law-enforcement people, the *blackbirds* aren't gonna sing on the Capitol steps."

The white citizens laughed, and rose to a standing ovation.

It is one thing to know that because of your color you are open game for mobs and spontaneous violence; it is another, deeper nightmare to know that the law enforcement agencies you must look to for protection are dedicated first to upholding the principles of your enemy, and only secondly (if it does not interfere with these primary principles of white superiority) to justice. Of course no Negro citizens were present to hear the heads of their city and state law-enforcement agencies publicly state their commitment to the protection of the white tradition, and specifically pledge that the police would see to it that Negroes would not be allowed to assemble peacefully on the steps of the statehouse. But the Negroes don't have to be told this; they know it from their daily experience.

The Rev. Robert DuBose, a young minister of the Episcopal Church of the Good Shepherd in Montgomery, had his own lesson in these facts of white law and order on the day of the Negro prayer march to the state capitol. Neither Rev. DuBose nor the other Negro leaders had any illusions about the dangers involved in staging this peaceful protest against the State expelling nine Alabama State University students who had taken part in sit-in demonstrations.

"Sullivan [city police commissioner L. B. Sullivan] said he would break up any march," the Rev. DuBose explained, "but we knew if we didn't do it that day, as we had planned, we'd have been licked. The church where we met was packed, and everyone who left the church with us after the meeting was ready for whatever would happen. We told them 'If you have a weapon, you're not ready for this.' All of us who left there were ready for anything; ready to go to death."

"The mob at Little Rock was nothing compared to the one that was waiting outside. When we got to the church before the meeting, the whole area around it was clear, except for newsmen and police. But between one and two o'clock, the police let the mob in. They could have been kept back where they were before, out of the area of our march."

"The police acted like a mob themselves—they pushed us and shoved us when we came out of the church. If they really had wanted law and order we could have had a peaceful demonstration. We marched several years ago protesting an electrocution, and at that time the police were there to protect—this time they were hostile."

When the Negroes came out of the church and

faced not only the mob but the policemen and deputies who stood between them and their march, they had to disperse, and many of them had cars parked several blocks away. The police refused to take them through the mob to their cars, and it was not one of the armed lawmen who escorted them safely through the angry crowd, but one local white minister who came to help.

After the prayer march, its leaders, including the Rev. DuBose, began receiving threats, and on the following day four white men were seen running out of Rev. DuBose's church. Fearing that a bomb had been planted, which is not an uncommon form of white retaliation in Montgomery since the days of the bus boycott, Rev. DuBose called the police.

"I told them I was a father, and I had a family to worry about," he said. "But although we called the afternoon it happened, the detective said we should have called earlier. He wouldn't send any of his men over."

There was no explosion, but Rev. DuBose and his parishioners feared that if the whites had intended to plant a bomb and failed, they might come again.

"We set up watches," he explained. "Our weapon was lights. We had flashlights and spotlights to turn on anyone who might come. A coward doesn't have courage if there are lights. We wanted to let the hoodlums know that the church was being watched, so I called the newspapers and the TV stations and I called the police detective to try to have him get it in the paper or on the air. But

nobody took it. One of the TV stations just
laughed."

Against the threat of violence, the Negroes must
depend on flashlights and prayers. Sometimes those
weapons are enough, and sometimes they are not.
There were a number of bombings of the homes
and churches of Negro leaders of the Montgomery
bus boycott (all of which are chronicled in Martin Luther King's autobiography, *Stride Toward
Freedom*) and their memories are still fresh. The
Rev. DuBose and his wife drove a visitor around
their city, pointing out the sights of interest, and
among them of course were landmarks of violence
remaining from the wrath of the whites against the
leaders of the bus boycott. Slowing down the car,
Rev. DuBose pointed out the house where Rev.
King had lived, remarking "See—the floodlights are
still up." Driving past another house, Rev. DuBose
explained that this was where a white minister
named Robert Gratz (who since has lost his congregation and moved on) had lived. Rev. Gratz,
one of the only white people to openly support
the bus boycott, had a bomb thrown at his house,
too. Rev. DuBose pointed to the lawn and said,
"You see that tree there? Bob Gratz planted that
tree in the hole that the bomb made." Montgomery
is a battlefield as well as a city. And in the battles
that erupt there, one side is armed and the other
is not.

The attitude of indifference or open hostility
to Negroes by the law in the South is of course
nothing new, and is not at all merely a result of

the Negroes' recent attempts to gain equality. The roots of this tradition reach back to the post-Reconstruction days when the Southern whites were taking back the power that the North had denied them, and taking it back with a vengeance whose principal victim was the Negro. W. J. Cash, whose brilliant book, *The Mind of the South*, remains the most eloquent and comprehensive study of the region, explains that after Reconstruction,

. . . with the gradual return of the courts to Southern hands, he [the Negro] was to become almost open game. For, from being places where no loyal white man could find justice, they turned now, and naturally, into being places where no black man would find it. In many districts, particularly in the deep South, the killing of a Negro by a white man ceased, in practice, even to call for legal inquiry. But wherever and whenever the forms were still observed, the coroner or the jury was all but sure to call it "self-defense" or "justifiable homicide" and to free the slayer with celerity. And if any black was fantastic enough to run to the courthouse with redress for a beating or any other wrong, he stood a good chance (provided he was heard at all) not only of seeing his assailant go scot-free, but of finding the onus somehow shifted to himself, of finding himself in the dock on this or some other count, and of ending by going away for a long time to the county chain gang and the mercies of persons hand-picked for their skill in adjusting his sense of reality.

The continuance of this kind of "justice" to our own time was shockingly revealed in the murder of Emmett Till, which awoke not only the nation but the world to the facts of white law and order in the South. Emmett Till was a fourteen year old Negro boy from Chicago who went down to visit his Uncle in the Mississippi Delta, and, because he reportedly whistled at a white woman, was dragged from his bed in the middle of the night and never seen again until his body was found in the nearby Tallahatchie River. But the horror of the murder itself was matched by the outraged attitude of the local whites—outraged not at the murderers of the boy, but at the widespread attention and headlines the murder had caused. The whites of the Delta could not understand why all this fuss should result from the murder of a Negro. As one of them explained to me over a coke in the drugstore at Sumner, Mississippi, as he nodded his head in the direction of the Tallahatchie: "That river's full of niggers."

When more than fifty reporters from papers throughout the nation and the world descended on Sumner for the murder trial, the people of the town were both angry and confused. At the lunch recess on the first day of the trial a county health office worker who had stopped by to watch the excitement asked a visiting reporter where he was from, and shook his head when the answer was New York.

"New York, Chicago, everywhere," he said. "I never heard of making such a mountain of a mole-hill."

The feeling that it all was a plot against the South was the most accepted explanation, and when Roy Bryant and J. W. Milam ambled into court in September, 1955, they were armed not only with their wives, baby boys, and cigars, but the challenge of Delta whites to the interference of the outside world. The issue for the local public was not that a visiting Negro boy named Emmett Louis Till had been dragged from his bed and identified later as a body that was pulled from the Talla-hatchie River with a seventy-pound cotton gin fan tied around its neck with barbed wire—that issue was lost when people learned that the world was clamoring to have something done about it. The question of "nigger-killing" was coupled with the threat to the racial traditions of the South, and storekeepers set out jars on their counters for contributions to aid the defense of the accused murderers.

Donations to the fund disqualified several prospective jurors, as prosecutors Gerald Chatham, district attorney, and Robert B. Smith, special assistant attorney general appointed to the case, probed carefully at every candidate for a day and a half before accepting the jury. Judge Curtis Swango, a tall, quietly commanding man, combined order with a maximum of freedom in the court, and when he had cokes brought in for the jury it seemed as appropriate courtroom procedure as pounding the gavel.

While the jury selections went on inside, the crowds outside the building grew—and were automatically segregated. Aging, shaggy-cheeked Anglo-Saxons with crumpled straw hats lined a long wooden bench. Negroes gathered across the way at the base of the Confederate statue inscribed to "the cause that never failed." The Negro numbers increased, but not with the Negroes of Sumner. A red-necked deputy whose pearl-handled pistol showed beneath the tail of his sportshirt explained that the "dressed-up" Negroes were strangers. "Ninety-five per cent of them's not ours," he said. "Ours is out picking cotton and tending to their own business."

Moses Wright, a Negro locally known as a good man who tends to his business, was the state's first witness. He pressed his back against the witness chair and spoke out loud and clear as he told about the night two white men came to his house and asked for "the boy from Chicago—the one that did the talking at Money"; and how the big, balding man came in with a pistol and a flashlight and left with Emmett Till. Mose fumbled several times under cross-examination, but he never lost his straightforward attitude or lowered his head. He still of course was "old man Mose" and "Uncle Mose" to both defense and prosecution, but none of that detracted from the dignity of how he told his story.

The rest of the week he was seen around the courthouse lawn with his pink-banded hat tilted back on his head, his blue pants pulled up high on a clean white shirt by yellow-and-brown suspenders. He walked through the Negro section of the lawn with his hands in his pockets and his chin held up with the air of a man who has done what there was to do and could never be touched by the doubt that he should have done anything less than that.

When Mose Wright's niece, Mrs. Mamie Bradley, took the stand it was obvious as soon as she answered a question that she didn't fit the minstrel-show stereotype that most of Mississippi's white folks cherish. Nevertheless, the lawyers of both sides were careful always to address her as "Mamie," which was probably wise for the favor of the jury, since a Clarksdale, Mississippi, radio station referred to her as "Mrs. Bradley" on a news broadcast and spent the next hour answering calls of protest.

J. J. "Si" Breland, dean of the defense attorneys, questioned her while he remained in his seat, occasionally slicing his hands through the air in the quick, rigid motions he moved with throughout the trial. She answered intelligently, steadily, slightly turning her head to one side as she listened to questions, replying with a slow, distinct emphasis. "Beyond the shadow of a doubt," she said, "that was my boy's body."

At lunchtime recess the crowds around the soft-drink and sandwich concession debated her identification of her son, and many were relieved in the afternoon session when Tallahatchie County Sheriff H. C. Strider squeezed his 270 pounds in the witness chair and said the only thing he could tell about the body that had come from the river was that it was human.

Sheriff Strider, who owns 1,500 acres of cotton

land, farms it with thirty-five Negro families, has
the grocery store and filling station on it, and
operates a cotton-dusting concern with three air-
planes, is split in his commitments in a way that
might qualify him as the Charles E. Wilson of Tallahatchie County. What's good for his feudal plantation is good for the county, and his dual role as
law-enforcement officer and witness for the defense
evidently didn't seem contradictory to him. His
commitments were clear enough that prosecution
lawyers once sent two state policemen to search a
county jail for one Leroy "Too-Tight" Collins, a
key witness for the prosecution who was missing
(and never found).

There were still missing witnesses, dark, whis-
pered rumors of fleeing men who saw the crime
committed, when Gerald Chatham tugged the
sleeves of his shirt and walked over to the jury
Friday morning to make the summation of the case
for the prosecution. Both he and Smith, who is a
former FBI man, had followed every lead and sent
state policemen driving through the countryside in
search of the Mississippi witnesses, but only two of
the four who were named—Willie Reed and Mandy
Brandley—were found. The time had come for
Chatham to work with what he had.

In a matter of minutes from the time he started
talking the atmosphere of the court was charged
with tension as he raised his arm toward the ceil-
ing and shouted that "the first words offered in
testimony here were dripping with the blood of
Emmett Till." The green plaster walls of the room

had grown darker from the clouds of the rain that was coming outside, as Chatham went on with the tones, the gestures, the conviction of an evangelist, asserting that "the guilty flee where no man pursueth," and retelling the story of the boy's abduction in the dark of night.

J. W. Milam, the bald, strapping man who leaned forward in his seat during most of the sessions with his mouth twisted in the start of a smile, was looking at a newspaper. Roy Bryant lit a cigar. With his eyebrows raised and his head tilted back he might have been a star college fullback smoking in front of the coach during season and asking with his eyes, "So what?"

When Chatham was finished, C. Sidney Carlton, the able attorney for the defense whose large, fleshy face was usually close to where the cameras were clicking, poured a paper cup of water from the green pitcher on the judge's desk, and opened his summation. He spoke well, as usual, but after Chatham's oratory he was doomed to anti-climax. There had been a brief rain and the sun was out with more heat than ever. Defense attorney J. W. Kellum, speaking briefly after Carlton before the noon recess, had the odds of discomfort against his chances of stirring the jury, but he did his best with the warning that the juror's forefathers would turn in their graves at a guilty verdict. And then he asked what was undoubtedly the question of the week. If Roy and J. W. are convicted of murder, he said, "where under the shining sun is the land of the free and the home of the brave?"

The question was a fitting prelude to the harangue of John Whitten, the defense's last speaker. The clean-shaven, pale young man in a neatly pressed suit and white shirt that defied perspiration announced his faith that "every last Anglo-Saxon one of you men in this jury has the courage to set these men free."

Mr. Whitten went on to declare he had an answer for the state's most convincing evidence— the ring of Emmett Till that was found on the body discovered in the Tallahatchie River. The body really wasn't Emmett Till, Whitten said, and the ring might have possibly been planted on it by the agents of a sinister group that is trying to destroy the social order of the South and "widen the gap which has appeared between the white and colored people in the United States."

He didn't name any group, but the fondly nurtured local rumor that the whole Till affair was a plot on the part of the NAACP made naming unnecessary.

It took the twelve jurors an hour and seven minutes to return the verdict that would evidently help close the gap between the white and colored races in the land of the free and the home of the brave. Tradition, honor, God, and country were preserved in a package deal with the lives of Roy Bryant and J. W. Milam.

Reporters climbed tables and chairs to get a glimpse of the acquitted defendants, and the newspaper, magazine, and television cameras were aimed at the smiles of their wives and families in a flashing, buzzing finale. Then the agents of the outside world disappeared in a rush to make their deadlines and the stale, cluttered courtroom was finally empty of everything but mashed-out cigarettes, crushed paper cups, and a few of the canvas spectator chairs that the American Legion had sold across the street for two dollars each.

Soon the crowds were gone, and the town went back to its silent, solid life that is based on cotton and the proposition that a whole race of men was created to pick it. Collections to defend the two accused murderers gave way to collections for separate-and-equal school facilities in Tallahatchie County, and four of the five defense attorneys returned every Wednesday at lunchtime to join the other Rotarians of Sumner in a club song about the glad day "When men are one."

Yet neither the people of Sumner, nor the people of the world outside, would soon forget what happened there. The name of Emmett Till became a symbol of the brutal results of the system of racial inferiority. But if anyone doubted that the system continued, in exactly the same spirit as the one in which Emmett Till was murdered and his murderers set free, those doubts were settled several years later. Not far from the scene of the Till tragedy a young Negro named Mack Charles Parker who was accused of raping a white woman, was dragged from his cell in a Mississippi prison while awaiting trial, and his beaten body was found in the river. Although the FBI investigated the case, and reportedly turned over a list of the members of the white mob that had murdered Parker, the State of Mississippi refused to bring them to trial.

Sometimes the passion and fearless defiance of Negroes carrying on the new revolt in the South seems hard for whites to understand. What causes a man to risk his life for the privilege of being able to sit where he wants on a bus, or buy a greasy hot dog at a dime store lunch counter? These protests are usually regarded as part of a battle for "first-class citizenship"; but the often forgotten fact is that in many parts of the South the Negroes are not yet treated as human beings, much less citizens of any class. The fight for equality on buses and at lunch counters are fights whose goal is not merely the achievement of the right in question, but rather the destruction of the whole system of inequality. That system is not just the code that prevents Negroes from going to white restaurants and theatres; it is the system that allowed Emmett Till and Mack Charles Parker to be murdered and their murderers set free; the system in which a Negro citizen doesn't call the police if a boy is dragged from his bed in the night by white men because the police are white too, and therefore the enemy. It is not really strange or remarkable that the people who are victims of such a system have begun to fight it with so little fear. They have, after all, nothing to lose.

Chapter II

The "Great Crusade" for Segregation

The home of Thomas Jefferson is just outside of Charlottesville, Virginia. Also just outside the town, in another direction, is the home of E. J. Oglesby, president of the Defenders of State Sovereignty and Individual Liberties—the Virginia version of the White Citizens Councils. In September of 1956 I visited Mr. Oglesby in the course of writing a story on the school situation in Charlottesville, which at that time was scheduled to become the first Virginia community to make a start toward integration of its public schools. The court order had been suspended, however, only a week or so before the term was to begin, and the segregationists were relieved and confident. Mr. Oglesby, one of their principal leaders, consented to give me his views on the future of the crisis if I would come out to see him.

Short and stout in khaki shirt and slacks that were decorated by a gold chain and a dangling Phi Beta Kappa key, Mr. Oglesby sat in a red velvet rocking chair in his living room, clenching a pipe in his mouth. He stated his credentials as defender of the people—native Virginian, head of the mathematics department at New York University from 1919-1931, professor of engineering and mathematics at the University of Virginia from 1931 to the present, and special teacher of actuarial classes at Prudential Life Insurance Company for twenty-five years (this latter position requiring thirty-six annual trips north of the Mason-Dixon line to Newark).

"You can," Mr. Oglesby assured me, "look it all up in *Who's Who*."

Thus established as a leading citizen, E. J. Oglesby, rocking gently and staring at the needle point message framed on the wall across from him— "God Bless Our Home"—proceeded to state his views on segregation.

"I figure it'll take about ten years to make the Northerners get it through their thick heads that we're just not gonna integrate. We'll keep passing bills and finding ways out. And if it comes down to it, we'll close the schools.

"This house you're sitting in right here used to be the Brookhill School for Boys—private school. It operated from 1857 to 1862, and then it closed down because the boys were all out busy killin' Yankees. We've got enough money here in this county to operate private schools for the whites. What the niggers are gonna do, I don't know. If we have to close the schools, of course, the nigger'll have to suffer from it—everybody knows that.

"Then, if the federal government says we have to operate schools, and operate integrated schools, we'll be ready to get out the bayonets. There were more Yankees killed in the last one than Southerners, and if they want to try it again, let 'em come on down."

Mr. Oglesby's prediction did not come to pass.

Although the following year his town indeed closed down its schools when the court order came, and operated temporary private schools in homes and churches, the year after that token integration based on a pupil-placement plan was adopted in Charlottesville. And when it happened, Mr. Oglesby and his troops were not on the scene with bayonets.

· The only bayonets yet to appear in the crisis of integration were the ones of the federal troops at Little Rock. The revolt of the white segregationists all across the South against the 1954 Supreme Court decision has not resulted anywhere in armed insurrection against the Yankees, and despite the talk of it from die-hards such as E. J. Oglesby, it is more than doubtful that it ever will. Harry Ashmore, in his book *Epitaph for Dixie*, tells of receiving a letter from a Little Rock bookkeeper who said that "If reason and ballots do not avail us in the end" the people would take up arms against the North. Mr. Ashmore comments that

> . . . when I look out the window of my editorial office, I gaze upon the bland stone façade of the local branch of the Federal Reserve Bank of St. Louis. And down the street I see the shining window that bears the sign Merrill Lynch, Pierce, Fenner and Beane. I can imagine many ceremonies taking place on the intervening stretch of asphalt—including a third term inaugural parade for Orval E. Faubus—but not my fellow townsmen lining up in double rank while the chairman of the

local White Citizens Council checks their ban-
doliers in preparation for a second march to
turn back the Federals at Pea Ridge.

But if the segregationists have stopped short of
getting out their muskets, they have tried about
everything else. And they have managed to inflict
a great deal of damage, not only on the cause they
oppose, but on the whole atmosphere of life in the
South, for Negroes and whites alike.

The most important and powerful organization
of the Southern whites who revolt against the threat
of integration is the White Citizens Council, founded in Mississippi and copied in every Southern
state (the groups in Missouri, Tennessee, North
Carolina, and Virginia have different names, but
almost identical goals and methods). The birth of
the Councils was the first answer to the call of
Senator James Eastland of Mississippi, who, shortly
after the Supreme Court decision was rendered,
declared that "We are about to embark on a great
crusade. A crusade to restore Americanism, and
return the control of the government to the people. . . . Generations of Southerners yet unborn
will cherish our memory because they will realize
that the fight we now wage will have preserved
for them their untainted racial heritage, their cul-
ture, and the institutions of the Anglo-Saxon race.
We of the South have seen the tides rise before.
We know what it is to fight. We will carry the
fight to victory."

In the face of the rising tides, fourteen men

met together in Sunflower County, Mississippi, in July, 1954, and formed the first Citizens Council. One of those original crusaders, a thirty-two-year-old, red-headed planter from Indianola, Mississippi, who had fought the good fight as captain of Mississippi State's football team not too many years before, is now executive secretary of the state council. The zeal of this man, Robert D. "Tut" Patterson, is not undermined by any thoughts of compromise. When asked what he thought about former Mississippi Governor Hugh White's estimate that integration was 100 years away, Mr. Patterson promptly replied, "I say 6,000 years."

Attorneys, bankers, planters, mayors, former local chamber of commerce presidents, and assorted school officials are among the civic leaders who have joined to help "Tut" Patterson hold back the flood. It was first reported that the councils, although definitely opposed to violence, would keep the land pure by "economic pressure." The idea of "economic pressure" provoked an unfavorable reaction in the press, however, and "Tut" Patterson then denied it.

"We do not recommend economic pressure," he told me. "That's false propaganda from the press. But of course we don't denounce 'freedom of choice' in business arrangements. If employers fire their help, that's their business." When asked what methods are used in the "crusade" if violence and economic pressure are not council weapons, Mr. Patterson laughed and said, "Would Montgomery Ward tell Sears Roebuck how he operates."

One tool used by the Jackson, Mississippi, council is a mimeographed "confidential communiqué" mailed to members. "Confidential Communiqué No. 14," dated August 22, 1955, gave information about a Negro named Arrington High who published a newspaper urging integration. The "communiqué" did not suggest any action, but merely reported the situation. Soon after that, Arrington High was asked to remove his money from a local bank, and windows were smashed in his home.

The councilmen assume no responsibility. They grind out the letters on the mimeograph and hope that hate and fear will do the rest.

It can never, of course, be established just which of the incidents that have occurred since the growth of the councils are results, direct or indirect, of council actions. The white front is so united in many Southern towns that the law and civic leaders are often dedicated first to their racial commitments and second to the duties of office. As the Mississippi Citizens Councils' Annual Report put it in reviewing the first year's accomplishments, "The idea of solid and unified backing of circuit clerks, sheriffs, and local and state officials in the proper discharge of their sworn duties was worked out."

This racial priority was evidenced at Sumner, Mississippi, when the prosecutors in the Emmett Till murder case sent state police to search a county jail for a missing prosecution witness. It was seen by a Southern reporter who went to Belzoni, Mississippi, in May, 1955, to investigate the murder of George Wesley Lee, a Negro minister who had committed the error of trying to vote. The reporter was given the names of four Negro witnesses. When he tried to find them he learned they were all in jail. The sheriff explained they were booked on charges of "stealing," although what they had stolen was strangely unknown.

But all this seems far removed from the chaste room in the Hotel Walthall in downtown Jackson, where much of the business of the Jackson Council and the State Association of Councils is carried on. There a tall, mustachioed man sits at a long metal office desk with a two-volume "works" of Thomas Jefferson on it and a wrinkled map of Mississippi scotch-taped to the wall above. The man is W. J. "Bill" Simmons, who prepared for the task ahead with a B.A. at Millsaps College and graduate study at Toule, France, and the Sorbonne. He, like "Tut" Patterson and three office helpers, is a full-time council worker. He is also editor of a Citizens Council newspaper.

The office in Jackson, like the one in Winona where Patterson himself holds forth, does not hope to bind the hundreds of councils into any hierarchy or strictly defined organization. On the contrary, the looser the network the less the responsibility the leaders need to take. Mr. Simmons emphasized that the state office has no jurisdiction over what local councils may do to help the cause in their own community.

This approach allows the leaders formally to disclaim responsibility for any group's actions—allows, for instance, "Tut" Patterson to say the councils don't use economic pressure, while at Yazoo City, fifty-three Negro signers of a petition for school integration in 1955 were refused the purchase of food supplies, lost their jobs, and had their credit cut off until all but two of the original petitioners removed their names. Petitions for school integration were filed that year in four other Mississippi cities—Clarksdale, Vicksburg, Jackson, and Natchez. Legal technicalities that nullified the petitions were claimed by the school boards, and names of the petitioners were published in local newspapers. No list remained with all of its original signers.

As unwelcome as the petitions were, however, the councils found that they served to awaken the whites to the "danger of mongrelization" (a favorite term of council propaganda).

"Our Jackson Council started in April, 1955, with only sixty members," Bill Simmons said, "and by mid-July we had 300. But after the NAACP petition was filed in late July we went over 1,000 in two weeks' time."

The action by the NAACP brought a similar response throughout the state, and by the end of 1955 the Mississippi councils claimed a membership of 75,000. The councils quickly discovered that their best recruiting impetus was provided by specific moves toward integration which aroused local citizens to the dangers in their own community. In a number of cases, however, plans for integration in schools in Southern communities have met with no organized opposition by the whites—and in these instances the councils often send emissaries to stir up segregationist passions and create a local opposition. They are often successful.

One of the first examples of this type of "Paul Revere" action on the part of the councils occurred in 1955 when Mississippi council members were dispatched to Hoxie, Arkansas, where school integration was proceeding without incident. Senator James Eastland himself led the group of white segregationists who called a rally at Hoxie to stir up local protest. The result of the meeting, and propaganda distributed by council members, was a hate-inspired resistance on the part of white citizens in Hoxie who had previously been resigned to the situation. Soon after the Mississippi council members had held their rally in Hoxie, the local school superintendent began receiving threats, and the school was forced to an early closing of the term.

These missions to whip up revolt in areas where integration is proceeding peacefully quickly became a standard part of Citizens Councils operations. Council officials from Mississippi have spread the word in nine other states, and the leaders of other Councils in the South commonly travel back and forth to kindle the flame of their cause.

In many cases, Council officials are "called in" to aid the battle in communities suddenly threatened with integration in one form or other. As it was learned in Mississippi after the NAACP school petitions, and in Alabama, where indifference to the Councils turned to zeal and resulted in a 60,000 state

enrollment after Autherine Lucy attempted to become the first Negro to enter Alabama University,
membership and interest rise in relation to the
threat of integration. And, too, this support falls
off during times of relative calm in the racial
struggle. It is hard to make any accurate numerical
estimates of Council strength because it fluctuates
so greatly according to the danger posed to segregation at any particular time and place. Council
membership rose to a new high in Montgomery,
Alabama, during the Negro bus boycott—but fell
off considerably after the Negroes won their fight.
As one white observer there pointed out, "A lot
of people figured there wasn't much sense in send-
ing their contributions and paying their dues to
the Citizens Council after it spent all that time and
effort in fighting the boycott and couldn't win.
Some of them just quit, and some of them joined
the Klan instead."

But whatever the specific numerical or financial
strength of the Councils at any given time or place,
their influence goes far beyond such statistics. The
fact that only some fifty people attended the Council meeting in Montgomery in April of 1960 to
celebrate the prevention of the Negro prayer march
on the state capitol is not so important as the fact
that its honored guests at that public meeting were
the top officials of the state and city law enforcement agencies. No politician in the deep South can
be elected without the support of the Citizens
Councils. Its platforms are decorated by Governors,
Senators, Police Chiefs, Mayors, and Congressmen,

as well as important business and civic leaders. If there are a few business and political leaders in the South who have refrained from open participation in Council activities and open endorsement of Council aims and methods, there are none who have spoken out against it—to do so would be to commit political, and perhaps even economic suicide. Most of the recently-elected Governors of states in the deep South—in particular Ross Barnett of Mississippi and John Patterson of Alabama —have been vigorous crusaders and star orators for the Citizens Councils. Older and more responsible politicians, such as Senators Lister Hill and John Sparkman of Alabama, have not raised the Citizens Council banner—but neither have they raised a peep in opposition to it. Probably the most ironic case of submission to the power of the Councils is the progressive Senator J. William Fulbright of Arkansas, who as head of the Senate Foreign Relations Committee speaks with one of the most "liberal" voices in Congress, but does not speak at all on the subjects of Governor Orval Faubus or the Citizens Councils of his home state.

With the notable exceptions of Ralph McGill of the *Atlanta Constitution* and Harry Ashmore formerly of the *Arkansas Gazette*, most newspaper editors as well have made their peace with the Citizens Councils. McGill is without a doubt the most articulate and outspoken foe of the Councils and rabid segregation groups in the entire South, and is heartily hated by the enemy. But Atlanta is by far the most cosmopolitan of all Southern cities, and most influ-

enced by the outside world—not the least by the
many businesses from other parts of the country
that have helped to make the city grow and pros-
per. This does not in any way detract from Mr.
McGill's courage in flaying the Councils and other
segregation groups, as indeed Harry Ashmore's de-
parture from Little Rock to work for the Fund for
the Republic does not detract from the tremen-
dously difficult stand he maintained there with courage and intelligence during the roughest days. The
point is that in practically every town and city in
the South the pressure of segregationist groups, led
by the White Citizens Councils, make any opposition to their cause a "practical" impossibility.
This does not of course mean that either newspaper
editors or politicians are prevented from deploring
the "extremists on both sides," for it can always
be assumed that by "extremists" they mean the
NAACP and the Ku Klux Klan—surely not the Rotarians, bankers, and Chamber of Commerce men
of the Citizens Councils.

The difficulty of making specific attacks in print
on the Council itself remains almost insurmount-
able. Of course a great many newspapermen sincerely believe in the Councils—but there are also
Southern editors who personally have no more
sympathy for the Councils than does J. William
Fulbright—and who take a similar stand of silence.
A notable case of the difficulty of a Southern
editor maintaining an anti-Councils position is found
in the history of Grover Cleveland Hall, the articulate and talented editor of the Montgomery
(Ala.) *Advertiser*. Grover Hall's father was editor

of the *Advertiser*, and won a Pulitzer Prize for his outspoken editorials condemning the Ku Klux Klan. When the Citizens Councils were born, Grover Hall smelled the same scent of Klan-like hate and oppression behind the Councils' façade of middle-class respectability. In a blazing editorial in 1954 Mr. Hall said, "The manicured Kluxism of these White Citizens Councils is rash, indecent, and vicious. . . . The night-riding and lash of the 1920's have become an abomination in the eyes of public opinion. So the bigots have resorted to a more decorous, tidy, and less conspicuous method—economic thuggery."

But as the pressures of integration rose, so did the pressures of the Citizen Councils—and at the same time, Editor Hall's criticism of them fell from the pages of the *Advertiser*. He turned his capable pen to recording the sins of racial oppression in the North in a series called "Tell It Not in Gath," and was quite outspoken in scalding the Yankee sinners. But he no longer turns his fire on what he once called the "rash, indecent, and vicious" ways of the Citizens Councils in his own home town and state. Yet the only way in which the Citizens Councils have changed is in their increase of power and influence.

One of the most significant effects of the Citizens Councils has been the success of the pressure they exert against any voices of opposition to their cause from within the white community of the South. The Councils have been a principal factor in the creation of a climate in which opposition or even questioning of their principles of white supremacy is equivalent to the darkest heresy. Council orators constantly compare the current threat to "Southern customs" with the crisis of Reconstruction; and the Council has been instrumental in reviving the rhetoric and attitudes of that era. In describing the atmosphere of Reconstruction in *The Mind of the South*, Cash wrote a passage that perfectly fits the situation today, especially in the diehard areas of the deep South where the Citizens Councils hold their firmest power:

"Criticism, analysis, detachment, all those activities and attitudes so necessary to the healthy development of any civilization, every one of them took on the aspect of high and aggravated treason."

It is a large order to expect a white population raised on the principles of white supremacy to suddenly accept the movement toward equality when they hear no voice that speaks in their own accents urging them toward the new position. Yet the threat of economic and political reprisal from the Citizens Councils have effectively throttled the voices of southern politicians and editors who could show their fellow whites an alternative to the resistance of the segregation leaders.

In addition to their key role in creating this one-sided climate of opinion in the South, the Citizens Councils have played a major part in filling that climate with the kind of hate and violence they publicly deplore. The results of mouthing a devotion to law and order one minute and stirring the passions of the crowd to an almost religious ardor against their opponents in the next was illustrated by the attack on the "outsiders" who attended the

Council meeting in Montgomery, and also by the fate of Arrington High, the Negro newspaper editor in Mississippi after the "Confidential Communiqué" reporting his activities. These are only typical examples of the kind of reaction that naturally follows the inflammatory council rhetoric in speech and in print that is not at all diluted by merely tacking on a pious declaration of adherence to "peaceful means" of action.

The Councils not only make a public show of deploring violence, but also of renouncing "prejudice" of any kind. But whether unwittingly or not, they have contributed to the rise of anti-Semitism in the South which has accompanied the rise of resistance to the threat of integration. One of the early dispatches "Tut" Patterson sent to his Council members suggested a reading list on the subject of integration which might well serve as a bibliography of anti-Semitic publications in the United States. It included such long-established bigot sheets as *The Cross* and *The Flag* of Gerald L. K. Smith, *Common Sense* of Conde McGinley, *The American Nationalist* of Frank Britton, and nearly all the other existent periodicals that preach a hatred of Jews and Catholics as well as Negroes. Mr. Patterson's purpose was of course to feed his troops all available information on the inferiority of the Negro, and these vulgar rags were probably the only thing he could find to support Council "theory" on race questions. In presenting them as recommended reading to all good Council members, Patterson noted that "Some of these groups are anti-Semitic; however, all of the religious groups—

including all Protestant, Catholic, and Jewish—have
been pushing the Anti-Segregation issue and it is
time for all of us to speak out for separation of the
black and white races, regardless of our race or
creed."

John Bartlow Martin, in his book *The Deep
South Says Never*, which contains an excellent ac-
count of the rise of the Citizens Councils, reported
that

> Today [1957] Patterson denies that he or
> the Council is anti-Semitic or anti-Catholic—
> many Jews belong to the Councils, including
> the Indianola Council, he says, adding that he
> employs a Jewish woman and formerly em-
> ployed a Catholic woman in his office. No
> doubt it is true that Patterson is not consciously
> anti-Semitic and that the Councils are not offi-
> cially so; so eager was he to get anti-desegre-
> gation material into the hands of his adherents
> that it did not occur to him to question the
> wisdom of encouraging the dissemination of
> anti-Semitic material. Today he is extremely
> sensitive on the question. Another Council
> leader has said, "I have the highest regard for
> Bob but when he started out in this he was
> completely naïve. He realizes the significance
> of anti-Semitism now. He was groping at that
> time."

But anti-Semitic overtones and undertones, if not
as bald as the attacks of the professional bigot
sheets, were a part of some of the early literature
of the Council written by its own members. One

of its first original publications was a pamphlet called "Black Monday" by Tom Brady, a Mississippi circuit court judge. In explaining to his readers the menace of de-segregation and the forces behind it, Judge Brady wrote that

> It is lamentable that attention should be called to the alarming increase of Jewish names in the ranks of Communist-front organizations of this country. . . . There are those today who would damn the Jew, who would like to see him persecuted because he controls the motion picture industry, the clothing industry, the jewelry market, and so on. His excellence in these and other numerous fields of business endeavor is the result of his own inherent intelligence and industry. . . . Because Arthur Spingarn is President of the NAACP it does not follow that all Jews approve of this rabid organization. . . .

Judge Brady, understand, is not condemning all Jews; merely calling attention to the lamentable connection between so many Jews and subversive causes. It is merely a danger to be kept in mind. As for Brady himself, and his Council colleagues, one might well assume that Some of Their Best Friends are Jews.

In recent years the Councils have been more anxious to escape the label of anti-Semitism, and are fond of pointing to their acceptance of Jewish members. Indeed, the Jew in the South may often join his local Citizens Council with genuine dedication—though perhaps not so much in the desire to protect the tradition of white supremacy as to protect himself and his family. This reasoning was well explained in an anonymous letter from a Jewish member of the Mississippi Citizens Council which was published in the April, 1960, edition of the Montgomery Citizens Council newspaper under the heading, "A Jewish View:"

> Because I have always manifested such respect for my own religion, my fellow members of my local Citizens Council would not for one moment entertain thoughts of turning the Citizens Councils' activities into anti-Semitic channels. This pattern is, I am confident, being repeated in all the towns and cities where respected and self-respecting Jewish Southerners have felt—as I feel—that segregation must be maintained and that membership in the Citizens Council will help to maintain it. I speak from first-hand knowledge when I say that there are many Jewish members of Citizens Councils both here and in Alabama. . . . The Jew who attempts to be neutral is much like the ostrich. And he has no right to be surprised or amazed when the target he so readily presents is fired upon.

But the target of the Jew is fired upon anyway, if not by the White Citizens Council he has joined, then by the Ku Klux Klan and local white Protestant hate groups that won't allow him to join. The Citizens Councils are by far the most powerful of the forces in the segregationist camp, but not the most "extreme." The difference in their attitude

to the Jews in comparison to the attitude of the
Klan is typical of the basic difference in approach
of the two organizations. The Councils alert the
community to the link between Jews and subversion, but admit that there are some "good Jews"
(those who believe in the principles of the Council). The Klan passes over such niceties of distinc-
tion and condemns all Jews—as well as all Catholics
and all Negroes. And it doesn't claim any devotion
to "peaceful means" in upholding its principles.

The re-lighting of the Klan's fiery cross in the
South would have seemed unlikely as recently as
five years ago, but now there are many thousands
of whites who have got out their old hoods and
sheets to march again. Even after the Supreme
Court decision, there seemed little chance of a serious Klan revival, for the "manicured Kluxism" of
the Citizens Councils had stolen the march, and was
generally accepted as the "modern" and more gen-
teel answer to the outdated spirit and tactics of the
Klan, which had long been condemned by the
South itself. Although there were small and scattered signs of Klan revival in the South after "Black
Monday" there was nothing approaching a widespread resurgence until after the Federal Government dispatched paratroopers to maintain integration at Central High School in Little Rock. Then,
according to one Southern observer, "organizers
sprang up overnight" throughout the South and
in a number of cities the Klan marched again, in
full regalia and considerable numbers. To the new
Klansmen it had seemed that the "manicured"
methods of the Citizens Councils were proving in-

adequate, and the whip and the burning cross must
be brought out again. The same line of thinking
set in this spring after the student sit-in demonstrations, and once again Klan strength quickly
multiplied. Today the Klan is a recognized force
in most of the deep South. Its acceptance once
again in the southern landscape can be seen in the
green and white signs beside the highway as you
enter Montgomery, Alabama, proclaiming the pres-
ence of the Ku Klux Klan.

But the newly-revived Klan is different in com-
position, if not in goals and methods, from its
earlier forms. As a secret white Protestant fra-
ternity riding during Reconstruction to take back
power from the Yankee-run governments and
courts, and mete out its own kind of justice, the
Klan was a kind of underground continuation
of the Confederate Army, and had the support of
most loyal whites of all classes. W. J. Cash explained of this early Klan that

> Its body was made up of the common
> whites, industrial and rural. But its blood, if
> I may continue the figure, came from the up-
> per orders. And its bony framework and nerv-
> ous system, the people who held it together
> and coordinated and directed it, were very
> near to being coexistent with the established
> leadership of the South. People of great promi-
> nence in industry and business, indeed, were
> often, though not always, chary about actually
> belonging to it, but they usually maintained

liaison with it through their underlings and the politicians. And its ranks swarmed with little businessmen. . . .

Today the "blood" and the "bony framework and nervous system" that once was the Klan's has been taken over by the Citizens Councils, whose leadership is, like the Klan's once was, "very near to being coexistent with the established leadership of the South." The present Klan leadership, as well as its "body" is made up principally of "common whites." The leaders of the Citizens Councils are politicians and businessmen of the Rotary or Kiwanis level of middle class society, but the head of the Klan is Eldon Edwards, a paint-sprayer in the Atlanta Chevrolet plant. Most of the upper and middle class supporters of the Klan deserted it in the mid-twenties, when its increasingly brutal tactics began to be condemned by most Southern politicians and editorial pages. It enjoyed a brief comeback in 1928 when it rode the tide of anti-Catholic sentiment stirred up during the Presidential campaign of Al Smith. But after that it faded from power, and was largely unnoticed except for a minor resurgence in the thirties when it marched in mill towns and industrial cities in the South to battle the threat of unionism.

In spite of the new and considerable strength of its recent resurgence, the Klan does not command the influence or fear of its former days of glory. Gone are its terrifying marches for vengeance described by Cash as the ". . . slow, swaying noonday parades through the burning silence of towns where every Negro was gone from the streets, and the Jews and the Catholics and the aliens had their houses and shops shuttered. . . ." A citizen of Montgomery described a march of the local Klan this spring by recalling that "When they marched in their robes and hoods up Dexter Avenue, the people simply stood around and stared at them. The Negroes paid no attention to them and the whites paid less. The general reaction was one of curiosity to see what kind of bird it was who would put on a hood and robe and march around on a Saturday afternoon." This kind of disinterested curiosity seems to be the common reaction to the Klan's new public parades. A Negro student at South Carolina State College in Orangeburg, S.C., explained that when the Klan marched through the town after Negro student demonstrations this spring, "We all went out to watch. There wasn't anybody hiding under beds like I guess they used to. Some of the students had cameras and took pictures of it. One fellow went right up and felt the material of one of the robes."

But if the Klan has not been able to recapture its old powerful and fear-inspiring role, its present reincarnation is still a force to be dealt with. Though politicians no longer lead it, they take its growing numbers into serious consideration in elections, and in deep South states they must reckon with the increasing "Klan vote" which, especially in the all-important Democratic state primaries, can be a determining factor.

In the atmosphere already established by the

Citizens Councils, which breed suspicion of "treason" and "subversion" in any failure to adhere to the line of white supremacy, the Klan is effective in scaring off any citizens from adopting "moderate" views or actions. The cry of "treason" and threats from the Klan, in cooperation with a small band of anti-Semitic, anti-Negro zealots in Montgomery, has effectively wrecked what few groups there were in the city which mildly promoted a less than Dixie-dedicated approach to the race question. The unaffiliated bigot group, composed both of men and women (female suffrage seems to be its main difference from the Klan) is centered around Rear Admiral John G. Crommelin (ret.), a former chairman of the Millions for McCarthy Committee, and a weekly newspaper called the Montgomery *Home News*. The paper is indistinguishable in its ideology from such sheets as *Common Sense* and *The National Defender*. But the difference is that this is a "hometown hate paper." You buy it on the newsstand, or in the hotel lobby. The degree of its acceptibility in the community (or, more likely, the fear of opposing it) can be seen in the fact that in its issue of April 7, 1960, eighteen candidates for political office in the city, county, and state advertised in its pages. Most of them alluded to their dedication to the cherished local customs, and John Crommelin, "the Whiteman's Candidate for U.S. Senate" was even more explicit:

As your Senator, I will ATTACK and EXPOSE the Anti-Defamation League of B'nai

B'rith (ADL), the malarial-mosquito of integration and REAL HIDDEN ENEMY of
White Christian Alabamans. THIS MUST BE
DONE. The ADL (all jew) is the mosquito;
the NAACP (jew-controlled Negro) is the
germ.

The followers of Mr. Crommelin and the *Home
News*, in cooperation with the Klan, succeeded in
breaking up an inter-racial prayer group of local
churchwomen in September of 1958. Many of
these churchwomen were wives of well-known
Montgomery business and religious leaders, and
they had been meeting for several years to sing
hymns, pray, and have coffee together. This inter-
racial conspiracy was wrecked when the local Klan
and their friends took down license numbers of the
attending ladies, took pictures of them as they
came out of the church where they had met, and
published their names and the names of their hus-
band's businesses in the *Home News*. The ladies
began receiving threatening and obscene phone
calls, husbands publicly denied approval of their
wives' actions (some took ads in the Montgomery
Advertiser, disassociating themselves from the opin-
ions of their wives), and the group has not met
since.

An even more subtle conspiracy was uncovered
recently by the Klan and the *Home News* followers. This was the establishment of a branch of
the Mental Health Society in Montgomery. Its
meetings at first were well attended, but then the
Klan and its friends turned out to picket and dis-

tribute literature explaining that "mental health" was only another aspect of the Communist-Jewish conspiracy. The aim of the Mental Health Society was to "brainwash" good Southerners into accepting integration. It was further revealed that these mental health people had a secret hospital in Alaska where Southerners were taken to have lobotomies performed on them which changed them once and for all into accepting communism and integration. To further prove the case against mental health, the picketers pointed out that most psychiatrists are Jews.

The people who had been attending the mental health meetings were probably not convinced of the logic of the attack on their society, but they were frightened by the KKK picket lines which greeted them before and after the meetings. Attendance dropped off until the society decided not to hold any more public meetings.

The end of communications, the beginning of fear, the nurture of hate for all elements uncommitted to a passionate defense of segregation, the breeding of suspicion of all who are not white Protestants are the fruits of the "Great Crusade" to preserve segregation. The membership of the segregationist organizations probably does not come near to adding up to a majority of the white citizens of the South, but their words and action control, manipulate, and speak for that majority. This spring the city of Birmingham threatened to sue *The New York Times* for two articles about race relations in that city, and its Chamber of Commerce asserted that the city was not, as a *Times* headline had said it was, "gripped by hate and fear." The majority of its citizens, the Birmingham leaders argued, went about their business as they always did, and were not at all gripped by hate and fear. I am sure that the Birmingham leaders were right—that the majority of their citizens were not "gripped" by anything at all. As Murray Kempton pointed out in his book on the thirties, *Part of Our Time*, ". . . the reality, as we know it now, is that most people are neutral." Just as the myth of the thirties was that every college campus surged with Communists and Socialists, the myth of the current struggle in the South is that every white is a passionate member of the Citizens Council or the Klan and every Negro a dedicated worker for the NAACP. The reality, again, is that most people are neutral. This does not mean that they don't have any opinion on the issue—it is certain, as proved by every vote for elective office and every public referendum in the South, that the vast majority of the whites favor segregation. But they are "neutral" in the sense that most of them don't care enough to actually join the battle. It is also surely true that there is a significant minority of Southern whites who favor desegregation, or at least are willing to accept it and try to make it work. But most of those citizens, too, fall in the classification of "neutral," for only a piddling few have spoken out in public. The segregationist orators speak unchallenged by their own white communities. That section of the white population that holds a different view has earned the label of "The Silent South."

Chapter III

The Search for "Moderation"

A year after U.S. paratroops had arrived in Little Rock to enforce the ruling which allowed nine Negro students to enter Central High School, Governor Orval Faubus met the beginning of the new school term by closing down the four public high schools and calling for a vote of public sentiment on segregation. On the day of the voting, I walked up to one of the polling places and was confronted by two stern men bearing a petition which demanded a recall of the local school board. I read the petition, and paused a moment. One of the men, evidently thinking I was a local citizen trying to make up my mind on the issue, leaned forward, squinting straight in my eyes, and said: "Tell me boy, deep down, what are ya—segregationist or integrationist?" The word "moderate," once a popular part of the Little Rock vocabulary, was now obsolete.

The man with the petition was probably right— "deep down" you are one or the other. The term "moderate," one of the labels most elusive of definition in the current civil rights battle, is usually most popular in communities which have yet to face a showdown on integration. As long as the crisis is yet to come, people can afford the luxury of the term "moderation," which is not exactly a flaming slogan calculated to inspire or offend.

But once the issue is at hand—once the school must be integrated and open, or segregated and shut— how does one exercise "moderation?" When the cards are on the table, you are, as the man says, either "fer" or "agin."

When a crisis occurs which requires a definite stand, the people who might have considered themselves "moderates" find that they quickly are shorn of that comfortable label. If they oppose the integration, they are then "segregationists." If they favor any particular instance of integration, they are branded immediately as "integrationists" or "Communists" (the two terms are often interchangeable in the Southern segregationist's dialogue).

This was the setting of extremes that prevailed in Little Rock during the public referendum on school segregation in September, 1958. With the threats and slanders of the several growing segregationist groups in the city, the possibility of leadership for public support of opening the schools seemed more remote than ever. In fact, the very notion of "leadership" had been made almost as obsolete as the concept of "moderation" by Faubus' tactics. The Faubus approach to leadership was explained to me admiringly by a local city official and friend of the Governor who said, "I talk to the Governor off and on, but he never asks my opinion on anything. A friend of mine is one of his chief aides, and he told me once the Governor never asks his opinion, either. When the Governor wants to decide on something, he gets in his car and drive around for a couple of days, just talking to people in gas stations and barbershops and places like that. He says if you really want to know what people think on something you have to sit around a gas station. Well, he does that, and figures out what the people want, and that's the way he makes his decisions. You have to admit, that's real democracy."

It might be easier just to make the gas station manager Governor, but the Faubus system probably comes to the same thing anyway. There is danger in proposing something that the people don't like, so the safest course is to find the lowest common denominator of what they do like and make that into policy. Leading the people is always more difficult than being led by them, and a lot more dangerous.

And yet, on this most dangerous of all issues, leaders of Little Rock who previously had kept their peace spoke out publicly in the campaign for the school-opening referendum. Even after Faubus had branded the Presbyterians who urged opening the schools on an integrated basis as "brainwashed" by the Communists, a Baptist and a Methodist minister, as well as the boards of deacons of a Methodist and a Presbyterian church, all came out with public statements favoring the opening of schools with the board's integration plan. Methodist Dr. J. Kenneth Shamblin discovered and quoted, in his sermon on opening the schools, that "Life is action and passion, therefore it is required of a man that he should share the action and passion of his time

at the peril of being judged not to have lived"—
a sentiment which more and more citizens of what
has been called "The Silent South" discover as the
crisis calls for voices. The Reverend Dale Cowling,
Baptist president of the Little Rock Ministerial Al-
liance, asked that his congregation "vote to keep
our public schools open even though this means
integration. I recognize that to do so may bring
us grave social problems. But these can and will
yield to a spirit of love and prayer."

These may sound like timid words to those who
can make fine moral pronouncements in the safety
of the North, but the Rev. Cowling probably understood, as he spoke them, what their immediate
effect would be on his church and his job. The next
Sunday, it was necessary for the Rev. Cowling to
deliver a sermon on the importance of church
members continuing to give their tithes and contributions in order for the church to keep up its
work. I sat in his church and watched the red
velvet collection plate passed down my aisle after
the sermon, and when it reached me, after passing
some twenty worshipers, it contained a single
nickel.

Later that afternoon I talked with one of the
Presbyterian ministers who, the Governor has
charged, was "brainwashed." This minister said
first that "I ask you not to print my name, because
if you did, the day that the article came out I
would be beseiged by phone calls, most of them
anonymous. Then I would be subject to new attacks and new reprisals from outsiders, trying to

undermine my congregation and their faith in me.

Since stating his own position in a sermon, in which he supported the gradual integration plan for Little Rock and said that the next step is for the Negro to have full political rights, this minister has not lost any members of his congregation. "But," he explained to me, "some have told me flatly that they will no longer give their financial support to the church. We ministers who have spoken out have jeopardized our positions, but we would do it again if we had it to do over. We couldn't do anything else. I have never been through anything quite like this in my life—my big job now is to try to hold my congregation together. And I think I can. I think we'll weather the storm."

Besides the ministers who spoke out before the vote on opening the schools, other local leaders even more vulnerable to economic reprisals took a public stand against the Faubus plan. (The best known and oldest instance of all is, of course, that of Harry Ashmore and the Arkansas *Gazette*, which lost 15,000 subscribers after it began to print consistently articulate and outspoken editorials supporting the school board's plan for gradual integration.) It was common talk in the community that several of the members of the school board had lost business for their respective companies because of their board membership, so the risks were understood by anyone who raised his voice. Yet before the voting, sixty-three prominent Little Rock lawyers bought an ad in the *Gazette* and signed their names to a statement that said the private-school plan would be illegal and urged the voters to cast their ballots "For Integration." One of the local segregationist groups, The States Rights Council, quickly issued a statement denouncing them and saying that "The people of Arkansas will long remember their names and in the future shun them like poison."

Perhaps the leaders who risked the most in making a public statement in favor of the integration plan were the local unions, for time and again throughout the state the unions have lost shop elections when management used the racial issue to dissuade the workers from organizing. But before the special school vote, state AFL-CIO chairman Odell Smith made a formal statement urging union men to vote for integration, and all of the local union leaders in Little Rock but one spoke up in their meetings to support this policy.

When the special referendum (which really, of course, had no legal bearing on the crisis in Little Rock) ended with a 3-1 majority for the Faubus segregationists, none of the millions of people throughout the world who were disappointed by the results were as deeply disturbed as those here who had worked for the opening of the public schools. And yet, there were solid gains made even in defeat that were bound to have a bearing on the future. As White Citizens' Council president, the Rev. Wesley Pruden, said when he branded the lawyers who urged the school opening as "political enemies" of Faubus: "They are so desperate that now they are coming out in the open." That was true, and it was also true that once in the open they were not so likely to turn back to sheltered silence.

A new group born in the desperation of the hour, The Women's Emergency Committee to Open Our Schools, decided after the voting was over that the referendum defeat for integration was not the end, but the beginning of their work.

The committee was formed just two weeks before the special school vote when Mrs. David N. Terry, a lady of one of Little Rock's prominent families, called together some friends to "do something" about the schools. The idea that women could do something in the crisis came from the memory of the women in Atlanta who formed a committee called Women Who Are Concerned and began the drive that eventually ended the sanction of lynchings in the South. These women of Little Rock were concerned, too, and after the first meeting at Mrs. Terry's home, fifty-eight women announced the formation of the new committee and began to contact their friends and neighbors to join in the work. Soon there were hundreds of women involved in the campaign.

The president of the committee, Mrs. Joe Brewer, a Little Rock citizen by birth and upbringing and a Smith College graduate, seems to embody the kind of dignity and grace that is the South at its best and is now its greatest hope. Faubus is Snopes and his kin are the majority; Mrs. Joe Brewer and the others like her, who are people of intelligence and principle, will always be, by nature, his greatest menace.

A few days after the sad results of the voting, Mrs. Brewer explained to me that "People have asked me if I wasn't despondent, but I'm really not —I'm glad about the response we got. I don't know how many women worked with us finally, but I personally talked to 250, and they all talked to others. And anyone who got involved with the committee knew there would be abusive letters and phone calls and that their husbands might be hurt in business. There's a lot of fear and hate here, and there's apathy, too—so many people say there's just nothing you can do about it. But we're going to continue to do everything we can. At least we've made a start now, and I'm sure we have a future. There are too many decent people here."

Mrs. Brewer said that in the short time since the committee had been formed, "So many people have asked me, 'Why didn't you get started a year ago?' Well, we should have. But when it first happened we were numb. And I guess we were afraid."

But because of the example of the mothers' group in Little Rock, similar groups in other cities have been formed before the battle. A group of mothers in Atlanta who had heard about the Little Rock Women's Committee formed a similar organization called HOPE (Help Our Public Education) almost as soon as a court order set the date for integration of the city's public schools. This spring Mrs. Donald Green, one of the mothers of the HOPE board, explained that "Since we started a year and a half *before* the shock of the actual date for integration, we hope we'll be able to save the day."

In their effort to keep the schools from closing when the integration date arrived, the mothers of HOPE held public meetings, circulated literature, sent speakers to talk on the issue before any group in the state, and for the first time brought the subject into the open. Until they went into action there had been no public discussion of the issue beyond the usual political oratory that "It can't happen here."

The HOPE mothers also made a firm impression on their state politicians. Once during every session of the Georgia legislature, the state's two U.S. senators return from the battle in Washington to give of their wisdom and inspiration to the troops at home, and in turn be duly honored for their latest forays against the federal menace. The occasion is usually—and especially in recent years—a time of rejoicing and rededication to the common cause of state's rights, segregation, and the preservation of the cherished Southern traditions. Standing ovations from the state legislators, as well as from the grateful citizens packed in the gallery, are a customary part of the tribute accorded the Senators. But in the spring, 1960, session, it was different. When Senators Richard Russell and Herman Talmadge made their appearance at that session of the legislature, the politicians rose and cheered as usual, but the gallery was seated and silent. It was filled with mothers from HOPE who carried signs that said "Save Our Schools."

Whether or not their efforts would save the schools from a shutdown, the mothers of HOPE had changed the climate of the segregation struggle in their state and shown the politicians that there was another force besides the die-hard segregationists. In explaining the group's work, Mrs. Green of the HOPE board said that "We've gotten help from the mothers in the Little Rock group, and mothers' groups in other states have asked *us* for help. There's a real feeling of fellowship among these groups in the South."

These groups of mothers protesting school closings are probably the closest thing to a widespread "moderation" movement on the race question that has come from the white South. But it is important to note that none of these groups take a stand *favoring integration*, but rather, opposing the shutdown of the schools. As a teacher from Virginia explained a 4-1 vote of the state Education Association in 1958 to keep the schools open, "There was a real unity among us all—but don't misunderstand. We weren't voting for integration; we were voting for public education." Nor does HOPE or the other mothers' groups take any stand for or against integration; they present the matter purely as a matter of schools or no schools.

This is of course practical strategy, and brings support from many people who wouldn't dare ally themselves with a group saying integration was "right" or "good" or desirable. But it again leaves the question begging of whether these people, or any other white Southerners, can be identified as "moderates." These committees only form when there is a definite threat to public education in their own community. The successful result of their efforts would be a token integration in the schools, and because they would rather accept that than accept an end to public education they are called "Integrationists" by the local segregation groups. But in attempting to define the term, can a person who does not take a public stand on the issue of integration itself be termed a "moderate" on the issue? Perhaps he can, merely by the fact that he has not taken a radical stand *against* integration. But this is indeed a rather negative "stand." It still leaves unsolved the search of Carl Rowan, a Negro who has won a high reputation as a reporter for the Minneapolis *Star*, to figure out the exact meaning of a "moderate" in the South. In his book *Go South To Sorrow* Mr. Rowan asks:

Who are these "moderates?" For what are they "moderate?" Are they moderately *for* or *against* compliance with the United States Supreme Court's decision?

After traveling all through the South in search of an answer, Mr. Rowan came up with his own definition: "Apparently a 'moderate' is any white Southerner who can prove that he hasn't lynched any crippled old Negro grandmothers during prayer-meeting hours."

The area of public support by whites for the principle of desegregation largely remains the No-Man's land of the South. There are, however, a few hardy souls who occupy it. There are men like Harry Golden in North Carolina, and P. D. East in Mississippi who put out small newspapers that sharply point up the nonsense of the complex prevailing customs of inequality. Yet sadly enough, both of these papers are mainly read in the North—and in fact, Mr. East does not have a single subscriber in his own home town. There are other scattered citizens who have already suffered so much, financially and socially, because of their views, that they prefer to remain as anonymous as possible.

One of the most notable of the Southern whites who has made his camp in this lonely ground is James McBride Dabbs, a tall, white-haired gentleman who wears a gold watch chain across his vest, and is, in accent, manner, and appearance, everybody's image of the Southern aristocrat. His book, *The Southern Heritage*, suggests in calm, carefully reasoned prose that the South must move forward to racial equality, and that it must now draw from the greatness and tragedy of its past the wisdom and strength to move ahead to the future. It is a book by a man who loves the South as his own land, and has searched its soul—as well as his own—to arrive at a reasoned plea for the acceptance of equal citizenship for the Negroes.

In addition to managing his plantation and writing his books (he recently completed an autobiography, *The Road Home*), Mr. Dabbs is president of The Southern Regional Council, one of the few and certainly the only significant, Southern organ-

ization which advocates inter-racial cooperation
and progress toward equal rights for the Negro.
The Southern Regional Council was formed in
1944 as an outgrowth of an older Southern organization called The Commission on Inter-racial Cooperation. The formation of the Council marked a
shift from the older organization's more paternalistic attitude of "doing things for the Negro" to one
of a cooperative effort between whites and Negroes. It is primarily an "informational" agency,
compiling facts and figures on the various phases
of segregation and civil rights in the South. It uses
this information to advise and inform interested
people, and Harold Fleming, its executive director,
travels extensively throughout the South, not only
gathering information but giving advice and data
to citizens attempting to make progress in race relations to aid the officials or citizens who are trying
to work for racial harmony. He and the other officials of the Southern Regional Council are, in this
sense, the opposite number of the Citizens Council,
whose emissaries go into communities attempting to
forestall any progress toward equality. But, unhappily, the Southern Regional Council is not in
any sense a "grass-roots" movement with the power
of the Citizens Councils. There are only a few staff
members, with headquarters in Atlanta, and much
of their financial support comes from the Ford
Foundation, in the North.

One of the significant results of the work of the
Southern Regional Council has been the formation
of inter-racial "Councils on Human Relations" in

local communities throughout the South. These local groups are an outgrowth of the SRC, though not officially a part of it. They are the only organizations in the South which bring together white and Negro citizens to discuss their mutual problems on an equal basis. They of course are small in number and in members. The difficulties that are likely to beset a white citizen who dares to take an active part in them are of course tremendous. These difficulties—even in an "enlightened" Southern community (this usually means a University town)—can be glimpsed in some of the troubles of Mrs. Sarah Patton Boyle and Mrs. Morris Brown of Charlottesville, Virginia.

"Patty" Boyle is a University of Virgina faculty wife who stands with enough credentials in the family tree to remove all suspicion that her ideas are a product of Yankee or "foreign" intrigue—and they rankle all the more sorely with the town's professional Anglo-Saxons because of that. Who among them had one of their grandfathers serving as a personal scout for Robert E. Lee and the other riding as Colonel under Stonewall Jackson?

Mrs. Boyle first became interested in Negro civil rights in 1950 through the case involving the entry of the first Negro student into the University of Virginia. Discussions with white and Negro leaders brought her to a new attitude on the whole question of the segregated South. "Up till then," Mrs. Boyle explains, "like most Southern whites, I had never talked with an educated Negro." Their side of the segregation story was a revelation to her, who had always considered the system "natural" before. Since that time she has written, spoken, and organized for the cause of equal rights in the South, and in February, 1956, an article by her entitled "Southerners Will *Like* Integration" was published in the *Saturday Evening Post*.

The title, which was not her own, and actually not a conclusion of the piece, caused almost more anger from Southern friends and readers than the text of the article itself. Her own title, changed for publication by the *Post* editors, was "We Are Readier Than We Think." "The best way to learn about integration is to integrate," Mrs. Boyle feels. "There are so many fears and illusions that can't be dispelled any other way."

Shortly after the 1956 appeal to delay integration in Charlottesville had been granted, Mrs. Boyle and Mrs. Morris Brown sat in the living room of the Boyle home and recounted the recent events to me. Mildred Brown, a tall, slim woman in her middle thirties, and the mother of a boy in the Charlottesville high school, had just been elected vice president of the Charlottesville chapter of the Virginia Council on Human Relations. Mrs. Boyle, a lively, graying woman in a lacy white dress and glasses that hang around her neck on a black ribbon, sat with a folder of notes and clippings on the coffee table in front of her. The two ladies might have been a committee for any town's Junior League fall program.

"I first got into all this myself after a mass meeting here in July to protest the integration," Mrs.

Brown explained. "Judge Paul had said he was going to issue the order for integration and a meeting was called by the Defenders of State Sovereignty—that's the group here like the Citizens Councils. Well, they say it was the biggest meeting ever held in town. There were thousands of people, and after it was over the leaders said that all of the people there supported the protest against integration. I knew I for one didn't support the protest, or what those speakers were saying. I thought if there were others who felt the way I did we ought to get together. I'd never met Patty Boyle but I knew about her article in the *Post* and so I called her up."

That was the beginning of the local chapter of the Virginia Council on Human Relations. The first meeting was held July 27, 1956, four days after the Charlottesville mass meeting. The new organization didn't draw the multitudes, but it did find sixty-nine white and two Negro citizens in the town who wanted to be members.

The Human Relations group drew up a letter to the governor deploring the outlay of more than half a million dollars in public funds in the battle against integration, and affirming that:

> We believe that desegregation can be carried forward in such a way as to accomplish better education for our total community and that it is the clear responsibility of the school board to immediately make plans to do so. This is a local problem and our community is capable of solving it.

The letter was adopted at the Human Relations Council's third meeting when the business was interrupted by the shouts of John Kasper. This was the young agitator out of Washington, D.C., Camden, New Jersey, and Columbia University who was arrested a week later and sentenced to a year in jail at Clinton, Tennessee, after stirring Clinton High School's first desegregated opening into a series of riots.

As executive secretary of the Seaboard White Citizens Councils, Kasper and his imported cronies worked three weeks in Charlottesville, but was unable to bring his own brand of Citizens Councils into being—a brand disclaimed as too radical by the Citizens Councils of Mississippi as well as by the local Defenders of State Sovereignty. It was not the voice of the Defenders, but of John Kasper of Camden, New Jersey, that shouted to the Human Relations members that "We in the Citizens Councils have declared war on you people. We're going to run you out of town."

It was the cronies of Kasper who set the big cross burning outside of the third meeting of the Human Relations Council and threatened Mrs. Morris Brown that there would be a cross for burning in her own yard. It was the people of her neighborhood in Charlottesville who gathered to defend her, a widow living alone with her children, the night the cross was supposed to be burned.

"Most of my neighbors aren't with me on my views about integration," Mrs. Brown said, "but no matter what their views were they stuck by me to see that there wouldn't be any trouble."

The cross wasn't burned that night for Mrs. Brown, but a week later the threat was carried out on another lawn. I was sitting in my hotel room in Charlottesville when the telephone rang and a pleasant voice said: "This is Mrs. Boyle. I just thought you'd want to know, there was a big cross burning out in the yard here tonight. Son took some pictures of it and then we put it out and brought it inside."

I asked how big a cross it was.

"Son? How big was that cross out there? 'Bout six feet? Yes, about six feet tall, I think. We're keeping it for a souvenir."

Mrs. Boyle and her friends felt that the cross was the work of Kasper's traveling agitators. The Charlottesville segregationist leaders are, of course, "respectable" folks, and had issued no official threats to their fellow citizens, black or white. Charlottesville is not Mississippi.

In Mississippi there is no Council on Human Relations. There used to be, but as Harold Fleming explained, "It became inactive because of the constant harassment of the members." The Council on Human Relations in Alabama has also become inactive. Its headquarters were in Birmingham, but the local police chief, Eugene "Bull" Connor, forbids inter-racial meetings of any kind. He does not distinguish between public or private meetings, and a gathering of white and Negro members of the Human Relations Council in the home of a member could be considered against the law.

Those Southern whites who venture into the land

beyond complete segregation or complete silence find that they have broken the laws of the prevailing social order, and, perhaps, the laws of their city or state. Whatever passion moves them to that No-man's Land can hardly be described as "moderation," which is not a passion at all. In the South, it is only an empty word.

Chapter IV

The Widening Gap

A group of undergraduate students from MacMurray College in Illinois, accompanied by their sociology instructor, his wife, and child, set out this year on their spring vacation for a "field trip" in the South. The purpose of their trip was not merely to study the race relations, but the politics and changing economic conditions of the region. The trip was also a vacation, and the tenor of its spirit can be imagined by the chorus of the song that some of the students wrote for the occasion: "It's hi, hi, ho, MacMurray's on the go!" One morning in the course of their journey they went to a cattle ranch outside Montgomery, Alabama. They came into the city of Montgomery afterwards, and met for lunch with some of the local Negro students and ministers in a private room of the Regal Café, a small restaurant in the Negro section. Someone saw the white students entering the Café with the Negro students, and the police were notified. Several police cars came, a TV reporter and cameraman followed, and the entire party was arrested and charged with disturbing the peace. The evidence rested on the fact that after the police cars and the cameraman and reporter arrived, a crowd began to gather. The judge found the defendants guilty, and ruled that the Illinois teacher and students would have to return to Montgomery to stand trial for their "crime"—eating lunch with Negro ministers and students.

They were apprehended under a new city statute that makes any action "calculated" to disturb the peace a crime; of course the arresting officers and the judge and jury decide what type of action is so calculated. This statute is the new weapon the city has devised to help maintain its complex customs of segregation. Before this, the city had passed a series of statutes outlawing a number of specific types of race-mixing—for instance, Negroes and whites playing checkers or dominoes together—but revoked them this year in the fear that they would be found unconstitutional by the higher courts. It is felt that the new statute on action "calculated" to disturb the peace can cover such threats to the safety of the city as inter-racial domino games, and at the same time have a better chance of standing up if challenged constitutionally, for it makes no specific mention of race.

So another piece of chewing gum is stuck in the dike that holds back the threatening tide. The segregationist may now sleep easier, knowing that a white man who sits down to have a ham sandwich with a Negro can be arrested and sent to jail for disturbing the peace. But isn't there any reason for alarm, even for the white segregationist, as he sees the walls between the races rise higher? Montgomery is a city of 70,000 whites and 50,000 Negroes; a city whose recent years have been scarred by bombings, and recently threatened by a mob, and whose Negro leaders have pledged their

continuing fight for an equality whose realization
stirs many whites to violence. Isn't it only practical
to establish some form of communication between
the races? I went with that question to Carl Bear, a
leading Montgomery businessman and an official of
the Chamber of Commerce.

Mr. Bear is a middle-aged man whose hair is
turning to a distinguished steel-gray, and whose
broad shoulders, firm jaw, and thin, straight-set
mouth, combine with his deliberate manner to convey an impression of rock-like solidity. Mr. Bear
looks like the kind of a man who, if he ever played
fullback, would not even bother to look for holes
in the line when he carried the ball. I began to ask
him some questions, and before answering he told
me to put my notebook and pencil away. He said
that after we talked I could write out some questions if I wished and he would write out the answers and send them to my hotel. The essence of
his stand—and of so many of his fellow white businessmen and community leaders—is most clearly
summed up in the written statement he subse-
quently sent me:

The relationship presently existing between
the white and negro races is substantially at-
tributable to the breakdown of communications between the races which occurred ap-
proximately four years ago following the bus-
boycott incident. Since that incident the only
voices which have been heard concerning our

social problems have been those of the extremists, or professional agitators, of both races who in neither case represent a majority of the white or negro community. I believe that essentially most of us, of whatever race, are men of good will and earnestly desire to get along with one another. However, there is a crucial need for the more emotionally mature and substantial citizens of both races to assert the leadership which good stewardship requires of them. In my opinion, most negroes of this community do not want integration; they do want equality, but they believe that equality can be had while the races remain segregated. They also realize that equality is a status in society which must be earned and cannot be accomplished by force, nor can it be conferred by judicial decree or legislative enactment. They know that this earned equality will require much more education, extending over a period of many years.

(signed)   Carl H. Bear

The exhausting revelation of this statement is that "communication" between the races means much more than sitting down at a table together. The heart of the problem is not that the white man refuses to sit down at the table, but rather that when he does, he refuses to see the real face of the man he is sitting across from. His whole life has prepared him to believe that the man across the table is good ol' Preacher Brown; and who can blame his blind refusal to see that it is Martin Luther King instead?

The main streets of downtown Montgomery come together in a quiet, sun-swept intersection that carries an aura of charm and well-being. A fountain sprays in the warm spring light, soothing music streams from public Muzak-boxes attached to light-poles, and the wide main street stretches gracefully upward to the alabaster columns and dome of the state Capitol, handsome against a sky of perfect postcard blue. In this peaceful scene stand the landmarks of conflict, past and present, whose turbulence seems too foreign to the setting. It was in this Capitol that Jefferson Davis took the oath of office as President of the Confederate States on February 18, 1861; a little below the Capitol's dome is the small frame building that served as "the White House of the Confederacy." It was here, just a block down the street in the Dexter Avenue Baptist Church, built by Negroes during Reconstruction, that a young minister named Martin Luther King, Jr., took over the pulpit on September 1, 1954. And it was here, in this same church, that several hundred Negroes assembled March 6, 1960, for their prayer march to the Capitol and emerged to find a mob of 5,000 angry whites. Montgomery is already known as "the Cradle of the Confederacy"; it is also the cradle of the Negroes' non-violence movement against segregation which started here five years ago with the bus boycott and now is shaking the South.

Surely the white people of Montgomery, who watched that movement begin, lived with it, and saw its success, should understand better than any other Southern whites what it's all about. But they refuse even to believe it. Five years after the beginning of the bus boycott, and less than a month after the Negro student sit-in demonstrations in public eating places throughout the city, Carl Bear can sit at his desk and write that "In my opinion, most negroes of this community do not want integration. . . ."

Martin Luther King, Jr., wrote in his book that, after the boycott was over, the Montgomery whites had a new respect for the Negro citizens. It is certainly true that the Negroes gained great dignity from what they did, and that by all rational standards the white people should have gained a greater respect for them. But the feelings involved in this conflict have little or nothing to do with rationality. Judging from the whites I talked with recently in Montgomery, the successful boycott did not increase their respect for the Negroes who carried it out, but, rather, increased the mistrust and hatred of them.

One might assume that even the whites who deplored the boycott might have at least gained a respect for the Negro's ability to organize and carry out a successful cause; a respect, in other words, for his ability as a resourceful enemy. But even this seemed to be lacking. I talked with a white reporter there who was not in any sense a rabid segregationist, but who nevertheless refused to believe that the Negroes had the ability to organize any kind of campaign. He said he doubted that Negroes would soon vote there in large numbers because "the Negro community just doesn't have the leadership to carry out a full-scale campaign to organize the voters." I asked if they hadn't proved such leadership in carrying through the bus boycott to a successful end. The reporter thought for a moment and said, "Well, that was different."

The sentiments of the majority of local whites toward the Reverend King and the leaders of the boycott are probably reflected with accuracy in the outrage vented on them by the press. To *The Alabama Journal*, Mr. King is a "despicable character." In denouncing the recent sit-in demonstrations, the Montgomery *Advertiser* had this to say about the Reverend Ralph Abernathy, who is now the head of the Montgomery Improvement Association (the Negro group formed by King to carry out the bus boycott):

Instead of diplomas and teacher certificates, they [the Negro student sit-in demonstrators] can mount in a frame upon the wall a picture of Dr. Abernathy jazzing around in his Gandhi impersonation for the TV and *Life* Magazine cameras, using them as potted palms in his act of aggrandizement.

Negro leaders like King and Abernathy are especially despised and ridiculed, for they are not the Negroes who fit the image of the shuffling old Uncle Toms—the image which the white so tenaciously holds to because it gives meaning to his whole rationale that the Negro isn't yet ready for equality, and is in fact genetically and educationally (or both) incapable of assuming the responsibilities of full citizenship. Part of the insistence by Southern whites that the movement for Negro rights is a plot engineered by outsiders (Jews and Communists) is based on the reasoning that the Negro is unable to carry it out himself. The emergence of Southern Negro leaders like King and Abernathy confounds the old comfortable theories —but does not disprove them to the segregationist.

Even today, the Southern white can say with conviction, along with Carl Bear, that the majority of Negroes do not want integration. How do they know? Why, they *asked*. I have never yet been in a city in the South in which at least one white person didn't explain to me that Negroes didn't really want integration; they had been assured of this only the other day when they asked their maid, or their yard man, who had been with them all these years and surely wouldn't lie. Perhaps the example that best explains the irony of these reports is one told by a white citizen of Montgomery who was present when the family maid was asked what she thought about the bus boycott. "Oh, my folks don't want to have anything to do with that kind of trouble," the maid had assured her employers.

"Me, I walk to work, and my brother Jim, he
drives and picks up some other folks and takes 'em
to work, and we just stay away from those buses
—we don't want to have anything to do with that
boycott."

Much is made of the genuine love that Southern
whites feel for the Negroes, and such love indeed
exists, as long as the Negro stays "in his place"—
which is out in the cotton field, mindin' his business and hummin' a tune. A recent editorial in the
Alabama Journal tells us how warm the feelings are
for those Negroes who stick to their cotton
pickin':

> One of the pleasant items in the day's news
> was a report made by the Negro county agent
> to the Montgomery County Board of Revenue.
> . . . Among specific individual reports was
> the fact that Minnie Guice of Mt. Meigs pro-
> duced the first bale of cotton in the county in
> 1959. . . .
>
> Outsiders are hard to convince that white
> citizens of Montgomery take pride in such
> achievements by Negroes who conduct suc-
> cessful farming operations and who are not led
> astray by the visiting agitators who come into
> the county to make trouble.
>
> Farm stories about our Negroes such as these
> reported by the county agent show how pleas-
> ant are the racial relations here when our na-
> tives are left alone by the troublemakers.

There are loving words for Minnie Guice, who
produced the first bale of cotton in the county;

but stones for Autherine Lucy, who tried to enter Alabama University. Despite the editorials of the *Alabama Journal*, however, Autherine Lucy is not going back to baling cotton; but it well may be that Minnie Guice's daughter will try to enter Alabama University. That is the terrible truth that the whites refuse to face, for it means nothing less than that the past they are trying to preserve is already lost.

That past held many genuine virtues—there were virtues indeed in the system of loving paternalism for the Negro—but it was mainly the whites who benefited from these virtues. James Baldwin reported in his "Letter from the South" that

... I talked to many Southern liberals who were doing their best to bring integration about in the South, but met scarcely a single Southerner who did not weep for the passing of the old order. They were perfectly sincere, too, and within their limits, they were right. They pointed out how Negroes and whites in the South had loved each other, they recounted some tales of devotion and heroism which the old order had produced, and which, now, would never come again. But the old black men I looked at down there—those same black men that the Southern liberal had loved, for whom, until now, the Southern liberal and not only the liberal, has been willing to undergo great inconvenience and danger—they were not weeping. Men do not like to be protected, it emasculates them. This is what black men

know, it is the reality they have lived with;
it is what white men do not want to know. It
is not a pretty thing to be a father and be ultimately dependent on the power and kindness
of some other man for the well-being of your
house.

There are many Negroes who of course still live
in that old situation of dependence and paternalistic
grace—but their numbers grow fewer every day,
and the attempt of the whites to preserve that dy-
ing relationship grows more irrational as it grows
more impossible. The Negro community of an entire city can band together in an unbroken boycott
against segregation, and still the whites can delude
themselves with the illusion that these same Negroes prefer what they fought to destroy. This
stubborn attempt to preserve the myth of the old,
dependent Negro who likes things just as they are—
the myth which is so essential to the rationale of
segregation—has many complex and powerful roots.
Certainly the whole area of sexual guilt and fear
is, and has always been, a potent and primary factor in the violent attempt of the whites to preserve
the status quo of segregation. As Mr. Baldwin observed, "The Northern Negro in the South sees,
whatever he or anyone else may wish to believe,
that his ancestors are both white and black. The
white men, flesh of his flesh, hate him for that very
reason." And in a conversation with a Southern
Negro Mr. Baldwin reports the uncomfortable and
little discussed reality that lies so deeply within the
heart of racial conflict and hatred:

"Integration," said a very light Negro to me in Alabama, "has always worked very well in the South, after the sun goes down." "It's not miscegenation," said another Negro to me, "unless a black man's involved."

This is not a new but a historic reality in the South, and is deeply interwoven with the history of the region. In discussing the extreme Jim Crow measures taken after Reconstruction, Harry Ashmore asks why these laws and their application pushed "the forms of segregation beyond anything that had been known or contemplated in the darkest hours of Reconstruction." He says that although there is no single answer,

> . . . there is a clue in the bombastic Southern literature of the period. It reflects a growing obsession with the sanctity of white Southern womanhood, and, by implication, a fear of "mongrelization." Miscegenation, it is true, was already underway on a grand scale in the region and proceeding at such a pace that a really black skin would soon be a rarity. Moreover, it was obvious that this wholesale crossbreeding was the direct product of the degradation that accompanies the extremes of segregation; whatever their desires might be in the matter, black women were available for the white man's taking. It was, however, a one-way traffic; the highest crime of all—beyond murder or treason—was the taking of a white woman by a Negro, and it made little difference whether it be by force or consent.

W. J. Cash, in proposing a theory of what he calls the "rape complex" of Southern whites, says that "Southerners felt . . . that any assertion of any kind on the part of the Negro constituted in a perfectly real manner an attack on the Southern woman. What they saw, more or less consciously in the conditions of Reconstruction, was a passage toward a condition for her as degrading, in their view, as rape itself . . ."

And that is what they see in the current attempt of the Negro to achieve equality. It is impossible to be in a Southern town or city for more than a few hours during any kind of racial crisis without hearing mention of sexual matters which seemingly have nothing to do with what is happening. On the night before the referendum on school segregation in Little Rock in 1958 I sat in a local bar and watched Governor Faubus discuss the issue. Several Little Rock men were sitting next to me, watching and listening very intently. When the Governor had finished speaking, one man turned to another and said, by way of comment on Faubus' message, "I'll tell ya I better never catch any nigger at *my* bedroom window." The other men nodded in affirmation. The Governor, of course, had made no mention of Negroes being at anyone's bedroom window. But the threat of the Negro at the bedroom door was what they had seen in the talk about desegregation of the schools.

These fears and unconscious motivations play a tremendous part in the rabid commitment to maintain segregation. But there are also some practical and very conscious considerations involved in the fight to preserve white supremacy.

An Alabama labor leader told me that he was convinced "that one of the aims of the Citizens Councils, and the more extreme hate campaigners, is the opposition to the economic policy of the AFL-CIO and the weakening of the labor movement in the South."

The threat that unions will mean integration has always been one of the major weapons of Southern management in keeping their workers from organizing, and thereby keeping down wages of both white and Negro workers. "Management can't go in and tell the white worker that they'll have to pay *him* more if Negro wages go up—so they feed him this social stuff instead—tell him that if he joins a union it means he'll have 'nigger officers.'

"The leadership of the Citizens Councils comes from the Chamber of Commerce, the landowners, the businessmen. This is partly an economic war for them. They need cheap labor—which means Negroes; any time there's a threat of an increase in industrial wages, there's a threat to their labor supply. Some of the leaders of the Citizens Council in Montgomery are contractors who wouldn't work a union man on a job. Most all their labor is Negroes."

When asked if the propaganda of the Citizens Councils had made organizing more difficult, the union leader said, "Oh, Christ, yes. In fact, it makes it more difficult to hold what you have."

There have been abortive efforts to form a white

"Southern Federation of Trade Unions," but lately
the talk of that has given way to intensive and
often successful efforts of Klan and Citizens Council union members to take over AFL-CIO locals.
"I've seen cases where they turned local union
meetings into Citizens Council meetings," the labor
official said.

The Klan and the rabid, less "respectable" Citizens Councils draw much of their support from
the white laboring class (paint-sprayer Eldon Edwards, Imperial Wizard of the KKK, is a member
of the U.A.W. local in Atlanta) and in many places
in the South they have turned union locals almost
into "branches" of the segregation groups. Efforts
of the international unions to remedy the situation
have been of little or no avail.

Harry Ashmore records in his *Epitaph for Dixie*
that

> In the last few years racial tensions have
> had an increasingly adverse effect upon or-
> ganizing campaigns. The union internationals,
> without significant exception, formally oppose
> segregation, and their charters declare their
> membership open without regard to race. The
> Southern locals, however, have been reluctant
> to follow suit; there is nothing in the act of
> signing a union card to cause a man to abandon
> the prejudices he has lived with all his life,
> and the unions recruit their members mostly
> from the ranks of the red-necks who nurse a
> special bitterness. It was no surprise that the

mob that chased Autherine Lucy off the University of Alabama campus included a heavy percentage of dues-paying rubber workers, or that there were Teamsters and railway workers among those present in Little Rock. . . .

The continuance of cheap labor in the South, which rests so heavily on the system of segregation, and the South's anti-union tradition is one of the major lures used to bring in Northern industry. And the absentee Northern owners—who control most of the industry in Alabama as well as in other Southern states—ask no questions about labor practices and make no attempt to interfere in the "local customs" of segregation. As the Alabama labor leader summed up their position: "They sit in their ivory towers in the North and their hands are clean."

Harold Fleming, director of the Southern Regional Council with headquarters in Atlanta, affirmed that the Northern corporations which are going into the South "have it within their power to make a tremendous impact" on the pattern of segregation.

For instance, Douglas Aircraft recently opened a plant in Charlotte, N.C., and went in with the understanding from local leaders that they would hire on a non-discriminatory basis. Few cities are likely to refuse the promise of a new industry that makes such a stipulation. But the Douglas example is one of a very few such cases. "For the most part," Mr. Fleming said, "the corporations that

come down here are interested only in avoiding
conflict."

That is an understandable desire, but even the
business strategy for avoiding areas of racial conflict is often based on a naïve view of the situation,
Mr. Fleming said. Businessmen tend to pick spots
where "everything is quiet" without seeming to
realize that today's "quiet spot" may be tomorrow's
explosion. A business might have chosen to set up
a branch in Mississippi, for instance, rather than
in Little Rock during the school trouble, on the
grounds that all was quiet in Mississippi. No new
businesses came to Little Rock during the school
crisis; now that it is over, the Little Rock Chamber
of Commerce leaders are trying to attract new
business with the line that "We've already had it
here; this is a safe spot to come."

Because of the profound effect of outbreaks of
racial violence in scaring off business from the
North, most of the bigger and more well-estab-
lished Southern businessmen have exerted important
pressure for maintaining order and squelching any
kind of mob action. Those who have a stake in the
economic benefits of maintaining the low-wage
pattern are well aware that maintaining civic peace
is much more important. No matter how attractive
the wage scale may be for prospective new businesses, they aren't coming into a place where there
are mobs and eruptions of racial violence. But the
pressure of businessmen in curbing such outbreaks,
important as it is, always comes as a last-minute
emergency factor. The Southern businessmen, like

their Northern counterparts, have shown little vision or initiative in planning ahead to create the kind of racial cooperation and progress that would prevent the threat of spontaneous eruptions.

It is unfortunate that more Northern corporations have not attempted to take fair-employment practices with them when they open branches in the South, for they are among the few "outsiders" who could make any dent in the local segregation patterns. With the exception of labor unions in some areas (this year, for instance, the North Carolina State Labor Council not only ruled against segregation in its locals but made a public statement supporting the Negro student sit-in demonstrations), the involvement and the influence of outside forces in the Southern crisis has been pitifully small. Yet the "Southern crisis" is, in the end, the American crisis.

It is, then, even more lamentable that the Federal Government, especially through the military forces, has not exerted the economic pressure at its command to bring about changes in local Southern segregation patterns. The economy of a great many Southern towns and cities is based on military installations. Although there is no segregation of the military personnel on these bases, Negro soldiers who are taken to Southern areas without, of course, any say in the matter, are asked to observe the segregated living customs of those areas when they go off the base. Yet the towns and cities are not asked to make any kind of concessions to the Negro servicemen who have to be there, and who are often accustomed to other ways of life. The kind of tension that can result from this situation was illustrated this spring when Negro airmen stationed at Biloxi, Mississippi, tried to swim at the local beach and a riot ensued. There were twenty-eight miles of beach at Biloxi, but no area on it where a Negro was allowed to swim. As a result of the riots resulting from the Negro servicemen's efforts to go swimming, the entire personnel of the airfield where they were stationed was confined to the base.

In cases of school shutdowns in towns such as Norfolk, where the children of thousands of white Navy personel were deprived of public education because of the local segregation squabble, the pressure of the Federal forces could have been used to influence the action of the community. The key economic role of these military bases gives them a legitimate power to exercise their influence in such situations, but they fail to do so. But it has been illustrated time and again that the force of the dollar is the one sure force that can be used successfully in breaking down local segregation practices. Harry Ashmore reported a typical case of what happens when outside economic pressure conflicts with local segregation customs:

> . . . the Mississippi Sovereignty Commission, brought into being by the 1956 legislature to keep the Magnolia State free from any taint of integration, and supplied with $250,000 of public money for the purpose, collapsed in its

first direct test against the outside dollar. The issue was the proposed erection of an $11,-000,000 Veterans Administration Hospital at Jackson, a facility that would accept white and Negro patients alike and house them together without distinction. "Well, we've got the Tiger by the tail," Governor Coleman said. "We either accept an integrated facility or we deny our Mississippi white veterans medical services they need." With only one dissenting voice the Commission voted to donate state land for the hospital.

Unhappily, the exertion of moral force on the South from outside agencies or institutions has not been nearly as effective as economic force. In fact, it has been of almost no effect at all. In many places, especially Alabama and Mississippi, the die-hard segregationists have seceded again, at least intellectually, from the rest of the country, and the attempt of national organizations which they are a part of to influence their actions on segregation has usually met with rebuff and withdrawal. This has been the case with churches in almost every instance. The formation of Methodist "Laymen's Leagues" in the South, particularly in Alabama, has been one kind of withdrawal of whites from the influence of their national church group. Another typical example of the church situation occurred while I was in Alabama this spring. The National Council of the Episcopal Church sent out an "advisory statement" urging support of the Negro sit-in demonstrations. The Rev. C. C. J. Carpenter, Bishop of Alabama, quickly issued a statement saying that Episcopalians in the diocese of Alabama should "ignore" the National Council's statement.

In the same week, the national board of the YWCA came out in support of the sit-ins; the Montgomery YWCA quickly met and issued its own statement, deploring the national stand. The local branch is now studying the possibility of breaking off relations with the national organization.

There is a tragic irony in the fact that as the Southern whites increase their own segregation from the outside world, the Southern Negroes become much more involved in the life beyond their communities. At the same time that the Bishop of Alabama was telling his flock to ignore the words of the National Episcopal Council, and the white girls of the Montgomery "Y" were considering cutting off relations with the national organization, the Rev. Ralph Abernathy was in Ghana, attending a conference on non-violent action, and Mrs. A. W. West had just returned from Washington to report to the Negroe's Montgomery Improvement Association on the recent White House Conference on Children and Youth.

"Don't worry about the Negroes here," one white Montgomery citizen told me. "They're doing fine. It's the whites you ought to worry about."

The white segregationists are not only drawing further away from the Negro, but also from the world beyond their own community.

Chapter V

The Revolt of the Negroes

A constant theme of Southern segregationists orators, waving the banner of states' rights, is that basic changes in local customs and traditions cannot be lastingly imposed from the outside. They are perfectly right; Reconstruction proved the point. They, as well as we observers in the North, forget that when we speak of The South (e.g., "The South Says Never," "The South Spurns the Court") we really mean the *white* South. This mistake in terminology allows us to overlook the fact that The South means Martin Luther King as well as James Eastland, and that the greatest pressure for change in the South today is not being "imposed from the outside" but is coming from within. It is the pressure of Southern Negroes to do away with segregation in all its forms, and its most dramatic and significant expression is the mass nonviolent movement against segregation that has grown from the Negro student sit-in demonstrations this spring.

On February 1, 1960, four Negro college freshmen sat down at a segregated dime store lunch counter in Greensboro, North Carolina, and refused to move until they were served. Within two months the sit-in protests had spread to sixty-five cities and every state in the South. The Negro revolt had begun.

Up till that time the Negroes' battle had been almost wholly centered on gaining equal rights through passage and enforcement of laws. The new non-violent movement does not of course mean an end to those important legal struggles, but rather a widening of the battle to include mass protests that may be against the law in Southern states and cities but will be carried on, as they have been already, in spite of illegality. "The greatest progress of the American Negro in the future," one of the new Southern Negro leaders said this year, "will not be made in Congress or in the Supreme Court; it will come in the jails."

This revolt is not only a revolt against segregation, but a revolt against the limitations and frustrations of the purely legalistic way of fighting it.

It is ironic that the white segregationists branded the NAACP as the most radical movement since the birth of Bolshevism, outlawed it in several deep South states as subversive, and generally regarded it as the greatest single menace to segregation. But to the Southern Negro students it was too conservative.

In the rhetoric that has made the initials "NAACP" sound to Southern whites like the trademark of the devil, the real nature of the organization and its leaders has been obscured. The Nation Association for the Advancement of Colored People has an inter-racial board of directors, and although its membership is open to people of all races, nearly all of its 320,000 members are Negroes. The Southern segregationists have stamped it as an "outside force," and in a sense this is true, for its headquarters and leadership are in the North. But half of its chapters are in the South, and its local Southern leaders have usually been the spokesmen and guides of their Negro community in any efforts toward desegregation.

I have met with the local NAACP leaders in almost every Southern town I have visited in the past five years, and have consistently found that their approach was marked not by the "radicalism" that they were supposed to be famous for, but rather, by a patient determination. While Charlottesville, Virginia, was drawing near to a court order for school integration and the head of the local segregationists was talking about getting out the bayonets for another Civil War, the city's NAACP president sat in his living room and told me about the relationship of segregation to world affairs. George R. Ferguson, the head of the Charlottesville NAACP, was the owner of a local funeral home, and the father of a teen-age girl who had hoped to enter the white high school that fall before the court integration order had been postponed at the last minute.

"We Southerners," Mr. Ferguson explained, "have to worry about our whole education system, regardless of white or colored. Virginia is ranked forty-fourth in education systems in the country. In the second World War they proved in tests down at Fort Benning that the Southern boy wasn't up to the Northern boy—races aside—just didn't have as good an education. What with Russia and

China coming up like this we've got to get to work and see each man develop his brain, Negro and white man alike—we're all Americans. I think there's no doubt that things will work out down here with integration. This is the atomic age; this is a new day."

During the shutdown of the schools in Norfolk, Virginia, I talked with R. D. Robertson, a business agent for the Amalgamated Meatpackers Union, who headed the NAACP chapter in his community. He told me that "We're not making any noise here—you won't see any 'statements' from the Norfolk NAACP chapter. We're just keeping quiet and going through the courts. We're just staying in the courts. We're going to wait till law and order prevail."

These are hardly the words of rabble rousers, by anybody's standards. They are the words of men who had waited a long time, and were ready to wait a little more, until the day when "law and order prevail."

But to the Negro students who started the sit-in movement, it seemed that the day would never come. Most of them were in elementary school, or beginning high school, when the Supreme Court rendered its decision against segregation in the schools, and many of them assumed that they would be able to finish their education in schools that were desegregated. They also assumed that within their own lifetime the other major forms of segregation would be destroyed, too, and they would be able to live as first-class citizens. But despite the brilliant and intensive campaign of the NAACP, despite federal court orders, despite, indeed, the law set down by the highest legal body in the nation, at the beginning of the sixth year atfer segregation in the schools was outlawed only six per cent of all classes in the South had been desegregated. And there had been no moves at all toward desegregation in Alabama, Mississippi, Louisiana, Florida, and South Carolina. By the going rate of progress (1% a year), it would mean that the desegregation of the schools would not be completed for 100 years. Segregation, even in the single area of public education, would then not be completed in these students' lifetime, nor even, perhaps, in their children's lifetime.

And the students had other reasons than the slow progress of school integration for doubting the triumph of law over customs of white supremacy. Probably the main area besides the schools where the NAACP had fought for equal rights was in voting. If not in the courts, then surely in the ballot box, there was hope for legally achieving first-class citizenship. Negroes all over the country were stirred by the plea for the right of all citizens to vote that was made by the Rev. Martin Luther King at a mass prayer pilgrimage to Washington in 1957:

Give us the ballot and we will no longer have to worry the Federal government about our basic rights.

Give us the ballot and we will no longer

plead to the Federal government for the passage of an anti-lynching law. We will by the power of our vote write the law on the books of the South and bring an end to the dastardly acts of the hooded perpetrators of violence.

Give us the ballot and we will transform the salient misdeeds of bloodthirsty mobs into the calculated good deeds of orderly citizens.

Give us the ballot and we will fill our legislative halls with men of good will and send to the sacred halls of Congress men who will not sign a Southern Manifesto because of their devotion to the manifesto of justice.

Give us the ballot and we will place judges on the benches of the South who will do justly and love mercy. And we will place at the head of the Southern states governors who have felt not only the tang of the human but the glory of the divine.

Give us the ballot and we will quietly and non-violently, without rancor or bitterness, implement the school decision of May 17, 1954.

Give us the ballot and we will help bring this nation a new society based on justice and dedicated to peace.

But even despite federal legislation to insure equal voting rights, great numbers of Negroes, especially in the rural areas of the deep South, were still deprived of their ballot in 1960. The Southern Regional Council has estimated that there

are about 1,200,000 Negro voters registered today
in the South, out of a potential 5,000,000. Naturally,
there are many who are not registered because
they haven't taken the trouble to use their vote. But
this cannot explain away the situation. If apathy
were the only barrier to Negro voting, then Governors and politicians throughout the deep South
would not have been busy this spring devising new
ways to keep Negroes from exercising the right of
the ballot.

The Civil Rights bill passed this spring included
provisions for federal judges to investigate denial
of Negro voting rights in areas where a pattern
of discrimination was established. If the court finds
such discrimination, it may appoint "referees" to
register the disenfranchised Negroes. Governor
John Patterson immediately went into conference
with his lieutenants over this threat, and local newspapers reported that the Alabama legislature was
planning to revise its congressional districts in order
to rule out the possibility of Negro majorities in
any one area.

Alabama had already experimented with such
tactics—and experimented successfully—when it re-
zoned the city of Tuskegee, drawing the majority
of the Negroes out of the city limits. To further
insure against the Negroes voting, the Board of
Registrars met in secret so Negroes wouldn't know
where to register. But occasionally the Negroes discovered them, so in 1958 the Board of Registrars
resigned, and no new board was appointed. Thus,

the faculty of Tuskegee Institute, many of whom have a Ph.D., cannot register to vote because there are no registrars in their county.

There are countless measures of harassment and intimidation used to keep Negroes from voting, and if one doesn't work another usually will. Today there are thirty counties in the deep South where not a single Negro is registered. Citizens Councils are often helpful in giving tips to registrars on how to turn down qualified Negroes—for instance, Louisiana State Senator Willie Rainach, a Citizens Council stalwart in his state, traveled around dispensing such information to registrars last year during his campaign for the governorship. The methods are often made up on the spur of the moment by the ingenious white registrars, however. One instance typical of the spirit of the questioning of the Negro voters was reported by a Negro school teacher in the deep South who was asked, supposedly to establish her literacy, to define the word "thief." She came up with a number of answers but none was accepted by the registrar. After telling her she had failed, the registrar informed her of the "correct" answer. "A thief," he said, "is a nigger who steals."

As Alabama State Senator Sam Englehart explained to the Federal Civil Rights Commission last year during its investigation of Negro voting rights, "slogans like *democracy* and *equality* and *the brotherhood of man* are fine in their place but they don't solve practical, everyday problems, and they're not going to solve this one."

The young generation of Negroes in the South were learning from their everyday experience that these "slogans" were indeed empty. They were learning that laws and constitutional rights were not bringing them the equality that they had expected to see in their own lifetime. They were ready for something more extreme.

In the atmosphere of violence and fear that existed in so many areas where Negroes were trying to win their rights, it would not have been impossible for them to resort to the violence and threats of their enemies, despite the consequences. Indeed, it might have seemed the natural thing to do. One of the most ironic cliches of the Southern conflict is the phrase "extremists on both sides," a verbal contortion which equates the cross-burning and violence of the Klan and the segregationist hate-groups with the legal measures of the NAACP. The best comment on this "equation of evils" was made by the brilliant cartoonist Jules Feiffer, who once drew a strip lampooning an Eisenhower press conference in which he had the President proclaim 'I am against extremists on both sides; those who want to bomb the schools and those who want to keep them open."

If the disillusioned young Negroes had adopted the tactics of the extremists on the other side of the battle, they would have taken up bombs and clubs. Instead they took up prayers and passive resistance. Some of the Negro students themselves have pointed out that of course when one side has all the arms, the only recourse left to the other side is non-violence. But in fear-inspired situations rationality doesn't necessarily prevail—and, in fact, one Southern Negro leader has proposed that the Negroes take up arms and "meet violence with violence." Robert Williams, the president of the NAACP chapter in Monroe, North Carolina, has publicly advocated this line of action. Williams was temporarily suspended from the Board of the NAACP after making this statement, but it was widely publicized, and could well have served as the rallying point for an armed Negro resistance movement. There could well have resulted a Negro counterpart of the Klan.

As a matter of fact, such a counterpart already exists, though mainly in the North. The Muslim Brotherhood is a militant Negro movement with a large following which preaches hate for all whites and the eventual "triumph" of the Negro race—by whatever means possible. The Muslims, too, might have served as the focus for the pent-up frustrations of a young generation of Southern Negroes who were promised rights that have rarely materialized. Fortunately for the South and for the nation, the students had another kind of example. It was extreme, it was non-violent, and it had proven successful.

The Montgomery bus boycott of 1955 had shown that the Gandhian methods of love and non-violence could be used, and used successfully, in America. The specific Gandhian influence in this social experiment and in the sit-in movements that copied its principles, have later been sometimes scoffed at. But the importance of that influence, and the way it shaped these mass Negro protests, can be found in the writing of the guiding spirit of both the Montgomery boycott and the student non-violent movement. In an article in *The Christian Century* entitled "Pilgrimage to Non-Violence," the Rev. Martin Luther King explains that as a theological student

. . . I had almost despaired of the power of love in solving social problems. The "turn the other cheek" philosophy and the "love your enemies" philosophy are only valid, I felt, when individuals are in conflict with other individuals; when racial groups and nations are in conflict a more realistic approach is necessary. Then I came upon the life and teachings of Mahatma Gandhi. As I read his works I became deeply fascinated by his campaigns of non-violent resistance. The whole Gandhian concept of *satyagraha* (*satya* is truth which equals love, and *graha* is force; *satyagraha* thus means truth-force or love-force) was profoundly significant to me. As I delved deeper into the philosophy of Gandhi my skepticism concerning the power of love gradually diminished, and I came to see for the first time that the Christian doctrine of love operating through the Gandhian method of non-violence was one of the most potent weapons available to oppressed people in their struggle for freedom. At this time, however, I had a merely intellectual understanding and appreciation of the position, with no firm determination to organize it in a socially effective situation.

When I went to Montgomery, Alabama, in 1954 I had not the slightest idea that I would later be involved in a crisis in which non-violent resistance would be applicable. After I had lived in the community about a year, the bus boycott began. The Negro people of Montgomery, exhausted by the humiliating experiences that they had constantly faced on the buses, expressed in a massive act of non-cooperation their determination to be free. They came to see that it was ultimately more honorable to walk the streets in dignity than to ride the buses in humiliation. At the beginning of the protest the people called on me to serve as their spokesman. In accepting this responsibility my mind, consciously or unconsciously, was driven back to the Sermon on the Mount and the Gandhian method of non-violent resistance. This principle became the guiding light of our movement. Christ furnished the spirit and motivation while Gandhi furnished the method.

That same spirit and method are the guiding forces of the student sit-in movement. The students take the principles of passive resistance with great seriousness, and in most of the places where sit-ins occurred the students held workshops and practice sessions on the techniques of non-violence. They

were aided by Southern Negro leaders like the
Reverand King, and representatives of the NAACP
and the Congress of Racial Equality (CORE). The
CORE organization is relatively small and had not
been well-known before the sit-ins. It was organized after the second World War as an inter-
racial pacifist organization, and, because of the experience of its leaders in pacifist activities they were
especially helpful in training the students in passive
resistance methods.

The student movement is also closely related to
the Negro churches, and many observers have won-
dered just how "religious" these young students
are, and what real role Christianity plays in it. One
of the practical reasons for the close connection of
the movement with the churches is the fact that in
most Southern Negro communities the church is
the main point of communication. There are few
Negro daily newspapers in the South of much size
or influence, and news and announcements are usually spread through the one common meeting place
—the church. The churches have been the focus
and meeting place of the local Negro civic organizations—like the Montgomery Improvement
Association which ran the bus boycott—that have
sprung up to provide leadership in many Negro
communities where the NAACP has been outlawed. The students naturally made use of these
existing groups and their facilities which were centered in local churches.

Of course a great many of the student demonstrators are deeply religious, and feel that Chris-

tianity provides the moral *rationale* and source of strength for their actions. But even with those students who are not especially religious, the Christian aspect of the movement has a "practical" application. As one student demonstrator, who had faced white mobs in Alabama on several occasions, explained to me, "When you see those white men standing there, their teeth clenched, hate all over their faces, clubs in their hands—well, you have to believe that *something's* going to help you. You almost *have* to believe in God." In the same sense that there are no atheists in foxholes, there are no atheists in the sit-in demonstrations.

The movement has only begun, but it has already made a tremendous impact. Harold Fleming, who, as director of the Southern Regional Council, has probably been in closer touch than anyone else with all aspects of the racial conflict in the South in recent years, told me in Atlanta that "Just as the Supreme Court decision was the legal turning point, the sit-ins are the psychological turning point in race relations in the South. This is the first step to real change—when the whites realize that the Negroes just aren't having it any more."

The leaders and representatives of the new generation of Southern Negroes who have shown that in spite of jeers, threats, jails or mobs "they just aren't having it any more" assembled Easter weekend at Shaw University in Raleigh, N.C., and affirmed that the movement they began with the lunch counter demonstrations was only the beginning of their struggle for full equality.

If there had been any possibility that the spirit of protest born in the student sit-ins that have broken out in every state in the South would peter out as a passing fad, there was no such possibility after this conference. The meeting, which was sponsored by the Southern Christian Leadership Conference (a new organization led by the Rev. Martin Luther King, Jr., and other young Southern Negro ministers) established goals, strategy, and lines of communication for the future in a series of discussions and workshops held by the students. Up to this point, the student demonstrations have been spontaneous; in the future they will not be. The students now have their own organization, which will work with, but not be led by, adult groups such as the Southern Christian Leadership Conference, CORE, and the NAACP, as well as local church and civic groups.

The question of the role of adults in the student movement was a ticklish one. Where many sit-ins have taken place, older Negroes have been skeptical and fearful of the results, feeling that the students were "going too far" at the present time. At a recent meeting of the Montgomery Improvement Association, the organization which carried out the Negro bus boycott, the Reverend S. S. Seay chided his fellow elders by saying that "A lot of our people don't seem to understand what the young people are doing—they say they don't agree with them. Well, that just means they aren't catching the significance of events—it's a case of intellectual sluggishness."

The conflict on tactics has actually been going on for some time throughout the South. In Atlanta, for instance, the local NAACP lawyer who had led the Negro community's battle for civil rights for several decades opposed a group of younger Negroes, in their late twenties and early thirties, when they wanted to boycott the city's segregated trolley cars several years ago. The elders felt that it wasn't the right time, but the "Young Turks" won out, the boycott was successful, and the younger men emerged as the more influential leaders in the Negro community.

The sit-ins have brought the students' feeling of protest over the adults' "slow" tactics into the open, and after some initial reluctance, most of the adults have gotten behind the movement with moral, legal, and financial help. The student action has, in fact, become a great source of pride and new morale for their elders, who have been in the battle so long.

Miss Ella J. Baker, executive director of the Southern Christian Leadership Conference, told the adults at the rally that "The younger generation is challenging you and me—they are asking us to forget our laziness and doubt and fear, and follow our dedication to the truth to the bitter end."

And King, in the evening's main speech, hit hard at the same theme, saying that the student movement "is also a revolt against the apathy and complacency of adults in the Negro community; against Negroes in the middle class who indulge in buying cars and homes instead of taking on the great cause that will really solve their problems; against those who have become so afraid they have yielded to the system."

The whole aspect of the "middle class" nature of this movement is fascinating and in many ways contradictory. For although it is a movement *against* the Negro middle class, it is against it because the students realize that the black bourgeoisie are not *really* middle class. They may have big cars, but they can't drive them to big vacation resorts. They may have fine homes, but they have to build them within the confines of the Negro ghetto. They may have good clothes, but they can't wear them to the best restaurants and theaters. The young Negro students, for better or for worse, want to partake of the real middle class values and rewards of American society. They want the same pursuit of happiness as the whites, and they want to be able to pursue it in the same way.

Naturally, the Southern Negro middle class is the section of the Negro community most often opposed to the new protest movements. They have the most to lose, at least materially. Many of them are in good standing with the whites of their town or city, and fear economic reprisals and the loss of benefits from subservient cooperation with the white leaders. In some cities, such as Savannah, Georgia, middle class Negro leaders have formed their own groups protesting the students' protest movement.

Because of its opposition to the Negro middle class, many northern liberals and left-wing sympathizers have assumed that the student resistance movement was ideologically committed to "proletarian" or "working class" political sentiments. These Northerners have often been shocked to find that the student movement is not at all a movement against American middle class standards and values, but rather, a movement to achieve them. One young liberal in New York City who had a student sit-in leader from Alabama as his guest told some friends in tones of awe and disappointment about his militant visitor, that "You know what he brought? *Seven suits*. He was only here for a week, but he brought seven suits!" The guitar-and-dungaree ranks of left-wingers will find few recruits among the Ivy-clad young Negro students, who are more likely to follow the economic impact of their demonstrations and picket-lines in the Wall Street Journal (as one older Negro journalist discovered with surprise) than in the liberal weeklies.

But whatever the long-range goals of these young people, their immediate aim is to break the back of segregation. And in their single-minded devotion to that cause, they have already given great inspiration to Negroes of all social levels and all ages.

Already, many Negroes who have known nothing but subservience to segregation all their lives have found new hope and courage in the students' example. Harold Bardonille, a junior at South Carolina State College in Orangeburg, S.C., was telling several students at the Raleigh Conference how the old Negroes from surrounding farms had come to

the college to offer their help when they heard
that police had broken up a prayer march by turning fire hoses on the students and had made mass
arrests.

"When they heard about it, a group of tenant
farmers came up to the campus," Bardonille explained. "And I mean these were real *tenant* farmers
—*dirt* farmers. You know? They went up to one
of the profs and said, 'What're you gonna do about
all those chillun that got hosed?' They said they
wanted to help, and they'd do anything they could.
They don't know what they can do, but they look
to us for leadership. They're eager to be a part of
this."

Harold Bardonille told the story with a kind of
awe, which was only appropriate. Those tenant
farmers in the depths of South Carolina are the
kind of Negroes whom King describes with the
lines of the Blues that say "Been down so long that
'down' don't bother me." But now even they are
looking up because a new generation has shown
them it is possible. To the students, in fact, it is
not only possible but necessary.

Camus wrote in his novel *The Plague* that the
people who risked their lives to join the "sanitary
squads" that fought the disease did so not out of
any sense of heroics, but because "they knew it
was the only thing to do, and the unthinkable thing
would then have been not to have brought themselves to do it." That is the spirit in which the
Negro students seem to have taken up their fight
against the "plague" of segregation. It seems so

luminously obvious to them that what they are
doing "is the only thing to do." Those students
who came from every state in the South to the
conference at Raleigh went about their business
with a quiet determination and a minimum of oratory; to look at the small groups of students scattered on the grass of the campus in the afternoon
workshop sessions, or seated in the humid class-
rooms in the earnest discussion periods, you might
imagine you had stumbled into an ordinary spring
day of study at any small college. In the breaks
between sessions the students smoked and talked,
exchanging news of what was going on in their
own school and city. Billy Smith, a student at
A & T College in Greensboro, was telling a Nashville student how he and his friends had been training the high school kids in the town to take over
the sit-ins when the college term ended for summer
vacation.

"They'll carry it right on till we get back in
the fall," he said. We can't let it stop just because
of vacation. We're ready to keep on going for five
or six years, or whatever it takes. This is no fad—
this is it."

And "it" does not mean merely the end of segregation at lunch counters. As Harold Bardonille put
it, "We're trying to eradicate the whole stigma of
being inferior." The lunch counter protest is only
a symbol of the students' expression that "they
aren't having it any more." Already students in
many of the cities have broadened their work to

include help in voting registration and preparation of economic boycotts among the adult community. Billy Smith said when he got to Greensboro that he and his fellow students would be starting a "door-to-door knock" in the Negro community to "inform them about 'selective buying.'"

The reports of the ten workshops that studied the major phases of the movement from "the Philosophy of Non-Violence" to "Jail *vs.* Bail" revealed the scope and commitment of the students' ideas. The young girl from the "Jail *vs.* Bail" committee reported quietly that her group's recommendations were that the students arrested in demonstrations receive no bail and pay no fines; that all persons arrested stay in jail. "This," she explained, "will show that arrest will not deter us."

One group of students studied the role of college administrations, and decided that Negro college presidents and administrators should back the students' action (at least to the extent of not allowing them to be expelled), and should be willing to do this at the risk of their own jobs. Most of the Negro colleges in the South are state-controlled, and have white boards of directors. Thus, many Negro college administrators who have expressed private sympathy with the student movement have had to maintain public silence—and, in the case of Alabama State, allow some of the student demonstration leaders to be expelled. The students at the conference expressed their belief that the college administrators should put the movement for equality above their own careers—as the students indeed have put it above their own education.

The workshop that studied the "interracial" nature of the movement (there were about a dozen white students at the conference from colleges in both the North and the South) recommended that "this shouldn't just be a movement for Negroes but for all people who are against injustice." The representative of the "Preparations for Non-Violence" committee stressed that only those who are certain they can meet the threats and violence with passive resistance should take part in the demonstrations, but that "for those who can't take intimidation, find something else for them to do— even if it's licking stamps."

The commitment to non-violence is a keystone of the movement, and the Negroes have learned its power and importance. At the Raleigh mass meeting, King preached the difficult text of this doctrine he has given them to use as their weapon against the ugly mobs they have faced already and will face even more often in the coming months and years. He said:

"Do to us what you will and we will still love you. We will meet your physical force with soul force. You may bomb our homes and spit on our children and we will still love you. But be assured that we will wear you down with our capacity to suffer. . . ."

That is the road they have set upon, and they have already passed the point of no return.